Contents

Introductory note	3
I. Struggles Against Fascism During the Depression	5
1. How the Silver Shirts lost their shine in Minneapolis by *Farrell Dobbs (from* Teamster Politics*)*	6
2. 50,000 anti-Nazis answer SWP call; 1,780 La Guardia cops protect Nazis *(February 22, 1939,* Socialist Appeal*)*	11
3. Should fascists be allowed the right of free speech? *(March 3, 1939,* Socialist Appeal*)*	14
4. Comrade Cross invents a problem by *Felix Morrow (May 1939 SWP* Internal Bulletin*)*	17
5. Resolution of July 1939 convention on workers defense guard *(July 7, 1939,* Socialist Appeal*)*	18
6. Proposals on initiating defense guards	20
7. Coughlin delivers fascist blast against workers defense guards by *Joseph Hansen (July 14, 1939,* Socialist Appeal*)*	22
II. Struggles Against Fascism at the End of World War II	24
1. Report on the Los Angeles antifascist campaign by *Murry Weiss (abridged) (August 1945 SWP* Discussion Bulletin*)*	24
2. Minneapolis picket line smashes fascist rally by *Barbara Bruce (August 31, 1946,* Militant*)*	35
3. Comments on the Minneapolis antifascist campaign by *Vincent R. Dunne*	37
III. Protests Against the American Nazi Party	38
1. Letter from James P. Cannon to Tom Kerry, June 23, 1960	38
2. Wagner hands Rockwell an issue *(July 4, 1960,* Militant*)*	39

3. No victory for Nazis — 40
by Joseph Hansen (March 6, 1961, Militant*)*

4. Letter from Joseph Hansen to Larry Trainor — 41
(February 6, 1961, Militant*)*

IV. The Struggle Against Racism and Fascism Today — 43

Free speech and the fight against the ultraright — 43
by Malik Miah (August 1975 International Socialist Review*)*

Appendix A: Selections from the Writings of Trotsky — 52

The danger of ultraleft tactics in fighting fascists — 52
(December 2, 1974, Intercontinental Press*)*

Background to Trotsky's Letter on tactics in fighting fascists — 54
by Gerry Foley (December 2, 1974, Intercontinental Press*)*

From 'The death agony of capitalism and the tasks of the Fourth International' — 56

From 'Why I consented to appear before the Dies committee' — 58

On the question of workers' self-defense — 59

Appendix B: From 'The Capitalist Witch-Hunt—And How to Fight It' — 63

Appendix C: An Example of Sectarian Adventurism in the Struggle Against Fascism — 65

Introductory note — 65
by Fred Feldman

No platform for fascist scum! SYL builds anti-Nazi demonstration — 67
(April 1975 Young Spartacus*)*

Defense of anti-Nazi demonstrators scores victory! — 70
(June 1975 Young Spartacus*)*

Illustration: Leaflet distributed before
February 20, 1939, demonstration — 15

Introductory note

The United States has entered into a period of deepening economic, political, and social crisis. As working people learn from bitter experience that capitalism cannot meet their most basic needs, the "rules of the game" of capitalist democracy will come under increasing challenge. The Socialist Workers Party analyzed this process in the main resolution adopted at its 1975 convention, "The Prospects for Socialism in America":

"This will inevitably lead to a sharpening of the American class struggle in all its forms and to deepening class polarization. While the tempo of this polarization cannot be predicted, its general features are clear. Millions of workers will search for the road to independent political action and will more and more turn to class-struggle methods. On the other hand, rightist demagogues and fascist movements, pretending to offer 'radical' solutions to the capitalist crisis will come forward as candidates for power" (November 1975 *International Socialist Review*, supplement to the November 7, 1975, issue of the *Militant*).

The main seedbed for rightist and fascist movements in the United States today is the racist offensive of the ruling class, which is aimed at reversing the gains won by Blacks and other oppressed nationalities in recent decades. The rulers also use the racist offensive to deepen the racial divisions in the working class, by mobilizing whites in defense of their special privileges. Examples of this range from the campaign to smash school integration in Boston to the union bureaucracy's defense of the use of seniority clauses to discriminate against Black workers.

The first signs of rightist polarization can be seen in the increased aggressiveness of the Klan, the emergence of new racist formations like ROAR, and the evolution of the National Caucus of Labor Committees (U.S. Labor Party) into a fascist organization.

A key to forestalling the future development of a mass fascist movement is the struggles against the racist offensive in all its forms. Ultimately, the only way to bar the road to fascism is to build a mass revolutionary-socialist workers' party which can lead the workers and their allies in replacing capitalism with socialism. Struggle against the small and uninfluential fascist formations that exist today should be seen in this context, and the tactics chosen must advance and not retard these broad objectives.

The past experiences of the Socialist Workers Party in struggling against fascist formations have great relevance as examples of the application of correct strategy and tactics in the fight against fascism. The axis of this strategy has been the concept of *mass countermobilization* of the workers and their allies against the fascists, through the building of united fronts. Experience has demonstrated that militant mass countermobilizations can isolate, demoralize, and deal damaging blows to would-be fascist terrorists.

This bulletin collects documents and articles on the Socialist Workers Party's approach to the antifascist struggle in various periods: the late 1930s, when fascist groups grew rapidly; the end of World War II, when they again tried to raise their heads; the McCarthyite witchhunt of the 1950s and its aftermath; and today, in the context of growing polarization sparked by the economic crisis and the racist offensive.

Appendices present selections from the writings of Trotsky and excerpts from the 1950 SWP resolution on "The Capitalist Witch-Hunt and

How to Fight It." By way of contrast, a third appendix reprints the greater part of two articles from *Young Spartacus*, the publication of the Young Spartacus League, a sectarian group which indulges in adventurist tactics in the name of "smashing fascism."

Introductory notes precede each section of this Education for Socialists Bulletin, providing historical background and other relevant information about the documents and articles that follow.

MAY 1976

I. STRUGGLES AGAINST FASCISM DURING THE DEPRESSION

The depression of the 1930s produced a sharp increase in demands for radical change. At first the combination of demagogy and reforms that made up President Franklin Roosevelt's "new deal" was able to assuage some of the discontent. However, when a slight economic upturn was followed by a new crash in 1937 and 1938, the conditions for a sharp radicalization existed. The labor movement failed to take advantage of this opportunity. Under Stalinist and Social Democratic guidance, the newly-formed Congress of Industrial Organizations (CIO) was politically subordinated to Roosevelt and the Democratic Party.

One result of the disillusionment with Roosevelt and the default of the labor leaders was the rapid growth of fascist formations. Among the more important were Father Coughlin's Social Justice movement and Frank Hague's dictatorship in Jersey City, New Jersey. These are described in the upcoming Education for Socialists bulletin, *What Is American Fascism?*

A third group which carried some weight was the rural-based Silver Shirts organized by William Dudley Pelley. The Trotskyists in Minneapolis set a good example by mobilizing the labor movement against Pelley's threatened attack against Local 544, the Minneapolis truckdriver's union. This struggle is described in the excerpt from Farrell Dobbs' *Teamster Politics* reprinted below.

Other fascist groups were inspired by Hitler's diplomatic triumph at Munich and by Franco's victories in Spain. The German-American Bund organized by Fritz Kuhn in 1936 was one of these. While it won some support, its direct association with Germany and German foreign policy, along with its crude mimicry of Naziism, limited its potential base in the United States. It was widely viewed as unpatriotic, and its leaders were held to be German agents.

Headquartered in the Yorkville section of New York City, the Bund attempted to organize a mass fascist mobilization at Madison Square Garden on February 20, 1939. This aroused widespread anger, but the labor movement and the Stalinists refused to mobilize against it for fear that a confrontation would strain their alliance with Mayor La Guardia. Under these circumstances, the Socialist Workers Party felt that even a small organization could get a mass response to a non-sectarian call for a countermobilization at Madison Square Garden. Leaflets and slogans were carefully formulated to appeal to the widest range of forces threatened by Nazi terrorism. The result was a mobilization of more than 50,000 persons against the far smaller Bund meeting.

Many liberals and Stalinist sympathizers tried to justify their refusal to participate in the antifascist demonstration by pretending that such demonstrations violated the fascists' right of free speech. This attempt to divert attention from the real issues was answered by an unsigned article, probably authored by Political Committee member Felix Morrow, in the March 3, 1939, issue of the *Socialist Appeal*. The article appears below. When a comrade interpreted the SWP's position as expressed in this and other articles as *opposing* the application of free speech rights to fascists, Morrow corrected him in "Comrade Cross Invents a Problem."

Stalinists also claimed that the purpose of the demonstration was to prevent or break up the fascist meeting. Morrow answered this in the March 10, 1939, *Socialist Appeal*: "Jerome's reference to 'forcibly' preventing the meeting is of course a dishonest subterfuge; the issue involved was that of a counterdemonstration, of mass picketing of the meeting."

A major part of the SWP's propaganda, agitation, and activity against fascism stressed the need for the labor movement to form workers defense guards as the key to successfully defending labor's gains and organizations against fascist attacks. A resolution adopted at the July 1939 convention on this appears below. The SWP took the initiative in forming defense guards in some instances. An example of the SWP's approach to building defense guards is reprinted in this section from the July 14, 1939, issue of *Socialist Appeal*.

Completely absent, of course, from the SWP's statements and activities in this period was any indication that small groups of radicals could effectively smash fascism or prevent its growth by launching physical attacks on groups of fascists. The key at each stage was the mobilization of the mass forces of the labor movement.

The opening of World War II and the end of the depression brought a sharp decline in the fortunes of fascist groups. The Silver Shirts virtually disappeared. Father Coughlin was silenced by the Catholic hierarchy. Hague went back to the "normal" methods of rule of a corrupt politico. Fritz Kuhn was convicted of fraud and deported to Germany where he died in 1951. Other leaders of the Bund were prosecuted during the war as German agents. The Bund was effectively crushed.

1. How the Silver Shirts lost their shine in Minneapolis
by Farrell Dobbs

The following selection[1] is from the eleventh chapter of *Teamster Politics,* a forthcoming book by Farrell Dobbs. The book is the third volume in a four-volume series. The first two volumes tell the story of how the International Brotherhood of Teamsters grew during the 1930s from a weak craft union to the largest labor organization in the United States. This growth was spearheaded by a militant Teamster organization in Minneapolis, under the guidance of veterans of the Trotskyist movement.

Dobbs, the key figure in the Teamsters' first over-the-road organizing drive, writes in this volume of the Teamsters expansion in the eleven-state area; employer-inspired FBI frame-up attacks on Teamster organizers; the Minneapolis Teamsters and Farmer-Labor party politics; and the struggles of the unemployed and the victimization of their leaders.

Besides its historical interest as an account written by a participant, the selection is of value for its description of the way an incipient fascist formation was fought off under Trotskyist leadership in an American city in 1938.

Special attention should be paid to two political aspects of the struggle that appear to have been virtually forgotten or to have been misconstrued by militants concerned over the threat posed by incipient fascist groups today.

1. The Trotskyists in Minneapolis did not make the mistake of attempting to engage by themselves in a physical struggle with the fascists or with the police detailed to aid the fascists.

In isolation from the labor movement, such a sectarian or adventurous move could have led to unnecessary casualties, and by its weakness, could have emboldened the fascists.

The role demanded of the Trotskyists, as they viewed it, was to help mobilize the workers through their unions against the fascist threat. Only an impressive action by organized labor forces could cut short the fascist bid for entrenchment in the city.

2. The Trotskyists in Minneapolis did not make the mistake of calling for violation of the democratic right of free speech claimed by the fascists.

As the Trotskyists saw it, the question of free speech was not involved. In a serious fascist mobilization, what is involved is the fascists' use of physical violence against their opponents as a step toward breaking up the labor movement, installing a totalitarian dictatorship, and ending all democratic rights. Fascist rallies designed to mobilize and organize reactionary forces go beyond free speech, falling within the framework of preparations for violent attacks on labor.

Consequently, the Minneapolis Trotskyists did not set out to restrict anyone's right to free speech, but to mobilize forces in the labor movement to meet the fascists on the ground they were preparing to fight on or had already begun to fight on in other parts of the United States such as Jersey City, New York, and Los Angeles.

The prime issue was to meet any fascist demonstrations of force by counterdemonstrations, which is also a democratic right.

From chapter 11 of *Teamster Politics* by Farrell Dobbs (New York: Pathfinder, 1975). This selection and the accompanying introductory note are reprinted from the April 14, 1975, issue of *Intercontinental Press.* They are © 1975 by Pathfinder Press, Inc. Reprinted by permission.

1. Anchor Foundation, Inc. All rights reserved. Printed by permission.

That was what the Trotskyists in Minneapolis sought to do; and how well they succeeded in doing it can be judged from the account given by Dobbs.

It might be added that Leon Trotsky, then in exile in Mexico, took a keen interest in these developments and considered the action in Minneapolis, like similar actions elsewhere in the United States at the time, to be encouraging evidence that the American workers might not have to undergo the cruel and bloody experience of a fascist dictatorship.

❧

Clashes between capital and labor in times of social crisis tend to stimulate activity among political demagogues with a fascist mentality. They anticipate that intensification of the class struggle will cause sections of the ruling class to turn away from parliamentary democracy and its methods of rule, and resort to fascism as the way to hold on to state power and protect special privilege. Each of the aspirants hopes, moreover, to be chosen as the "fuehrer" to lead the terrorist movement needed for the murderous assault on the working class that accompanies such a turn in policy.

Several of these would-be Hitlers had, in fact, come forward in this country in the early 1930s, but they made little headway in the period marked by the stormy rise of the CIO. Then, during 1937–38, the situation began to change. A second deep economic slump developed, marking the collapse of Roosevelt's New Deal. Social contradictions in general grew sharper, as the ruling class prepared to plunge the country into the impending imperialist war. The bureaucratic misleaders in the trade unions failed to guide the workers toward a meaningful course for coping with difficulties caused by these developments—formation of an independent labor party. And in those circumstances significant numbers of demoralized middle-class elements in the cities, impoverished farmers, and to a certain extent unemployed workers fell prey to ultraright hucksters.

As a result various profascist groups that had sprung up earlier began to recruit quite rapidly, and they received a parallel increase in financial backing from wealthy antilabor interests. Emboldened by this new support, they became more aggressive, as well as more provocative. In some instances these outfits organized uniformed bands of storm troopers, which were drilled openly; and whether uniformed or not, thugs of that type were mobilized to launch terror campaigns, initially directed at the most vulnerable targets, but aimed basically at organized labor.

Jewish people were among the first to be attacked. As in Nazi Germany, they were made scapegoats in an effort to intensify anti-Semitic prejudices against them, the primary object being to sow division in the working class. But they weren't the only victims.

Lone worker-militants were waylaid and beaten in New York and other eastern cities. Street meetings of left-wing groups were broken up. In Jersey City the notorious Mayor Frank Hague engineered hoodlum assaults on union meetings and picket lines; and in New Orleans a Teamster strike was crushed by vigilantes. As the latter events showed, the ultraright forces that were engaged in these terrorist acts on behalf of the capitalists were rapidly zeroing in on their main target—the mass organizations of the working class.

One of these profascist groups, the Silver Shirts of America, was of special concern to General Drivers Union, Local 544. It was started in 1932 by William Dudley Pelley, who opened a headquarters in Asheville, North Carolina, and published a weekly organ called *Liberation*. Tacitly conceding jurisdiction over the major cities to other ultrarightists, Pelley centered his efforts on the towns and countryside of the farming areas. Although little was achieved in that sphere during the first years, the Silver Shirts had at last begun to make gains.

Apparently this caused a section of the boss class in Minneapolis to become interested in the movement; and Pelley was encouraged to send one of his aides, Roy Zachary, to the city in the summer of 1938 to launch an organizing drive. Two Silver Shirt rallies followed in quick succession, on July 29 and August 2, at the Royal Arcanum hall. These affairs were closed to the public, admission being by invitation only.

Despite the secrecy, the Teamsters had gotten wind of Zachary's arrival in town and had kept him under close scrutiny. Knowledge of the planned rallies was gained beforehand, making it possible to arrange a way to get reliable intelligence as to what happened.

Thus it became known immediately that Zachary's main theme had been to call for a vigilante attack on the headquarters of Local 544.

It was also learned that literature was passed out at both meetings inviting the participants to join F.L. Taylor's "Associated Council of Independent Unions." Taylor, by the way, had already shown his fascist inclinations a few weeks earlier when he set out to form a vigilante force under the name "Minnesota Minute Men." So it was perfectly natural for him to hook up with the Silver Shirts when they moved in.

A short time later another ominous fact was revealed by Rabbi Gordon, a religious opponent of fascism, who had also been keeping track of Zachary's doings. Gordon announced that George K. Belden, head of the Associated Industries, had attended both Silver Shirt rallies. When questioned about this by the press, Belden told a reporter for the *Minnesota Leader:* "I am in sympathy with getting rid of racketeers. . . ."

Taken as a whole, these developments added up to a dire threat against the Teamsters. The fink union, which had dragged Local 544 into court,[2] was now tied in with the Silver Shirts; Belden's role showed that the employers were directly involved in the new antiunion plot; and talk of an armed raid on the Teamster headquarters was in the air.

This situation called for prompt countermeasures. So Local 544, acting with its customary decisiveness, answered the threat by organizing a union defense guard during August 1938.

Formation of the guard was reported in the *Northwest Organizer,* and a press release announcing the step was handed to the daily papers, which gave it prominent mention. The new body's functions were described in the report as "defense of the union's picket lines, headquarters and members against anti-labor violence." Through this action the local served public notice that it would take care of its own defense, putting no misplaced reliance on the police for protection.

The union leaders were fully aware that capitalist politicians in seats of power not only tend to wink at fascist hooliganism; they often encourage and abet such extralegal attacks on workers. Not only that. Their minions, the police, condone and protect fascist activities, become members of such movements and, when open violence is used against the trade unions, usually look the other way. Such had been the conduct of capitalist "forces of law and order" in Germany, Italy, and other places; history taught that the situation would be no different in the United States.

An iron necessity was thus imposed upon the workers. If they were to defend themselves, they had to use their own organizations for the purpose. In that respect Local 544's pioneer action in forming a union defense guard not only served its own needs; the step blazed a trail for trade unionists everywhere in the country.

Conceptually, the guard was not envisaged as the narrow formation of a single union. It was viewed rather as the nucleus around which to build the broadest possible united defense movement. From the outset, efforts were made to involve other unions in the project. It was expected that time and events could also make it possible to extend the united front to include the unemployed, minority peoples, youth—all potential victims of the fascists, vigilantes, or other reactionaries.

For these reasons the defense formation was not made an official part of Local 544. Instead, it was initiated by leading members of the local, acting with the approval of the general membership. A spontaneous recruitment process was set into motion through a series of meetings with groups of workers. In this way the main base of the guard was quickly established by the General Drivers; and after that its ranks were gradually extended to include members of other unions in the city that approved the idea.

The guard was in no sense an elite body. It was simply a businesslike formation open to any active union member. The only requirements for inclusion in its ranks were readiness to defend the unions from attack, willingness to take the necessary training for that purpose, and acceptance of the democratic discipline required in a combat unit. Moreover, its activities were conducted only

---

2. The court action mentioned here was a suit filed against the officers of Local 544 by five members of the "Associated Council of Independent Unions." Without citing evidence, the plaintiffs charged Local 544 leaders with shady financial dealings and "conspiracy in restraint of trade." Local 544 waged a vigorous defense campaign against this suit and the threat of government intervention that it entailed. Chapter 10 of *Teamster Politics* describes this suit in greater detail.—*IP*

with the consent of the membership of the trade unions involved, and under their control.

As in the case of Local 544 itself, the guard functioned democratically in its internal affairs. Steps taken to carry out its assigned tasks were decided through open discussion and majority vote. This procedure was also used in selecting leaders who were to have command authority during any combat.

Ray Rainbolt of the Local 544 staff was elected commander in chief of the defense formation. He had impressive credentials. Besides his extensive know-how in leading trade-union struggles, he had acquired considerable military knowledge during earlier hitches in the U.S. army.

Those chosen as lower-ranking officers had likewise proven themselves in the class struggle and won recognition as secondary union leaders. Similarly, in the case of the guard's rank and file, all had been battle tested to one extent or another in strike actions. Taking the body as a whole, there were numerous military veterans with various abilities developed in the armed forces. Among them were former sharpshooters, machine gunners, tank operators, and so on. Quite a few had been noncommissioned officers. One had been a signal corps officer and still another an officer in the German army.

Structurally, the body was divided into small units to facilitate rapid mobilization in the event of a surprise attack on the union movement. Squads of five were the norm, with a member of each squad being designated captain. In a relatively short time the force thus organized was built up to about 600.

Members of the guard were issued small lapel emblems bearing the legend "544 UDG," which they were encouraged to wear at all times. When on duty they used large armbands prominently marked "544 Union Defense Guard" to identify themselves. This designation was readily accepted by those from other unions who were part of the formation, because they realized that use of the prestigious number 544 gave the name added meaning.

The organization raised its own funds—for purchases of equipment and to meet general expenses—by sponsoring dances and other social affairs. Part of this money was used to buy two .22 caliber target pistols and two .22 caliber rifles to give guard members a way to improve their ability to shoot straight. Regular practice sessions were then held for that purpose. In addition, periodic drills were scheduled to provide training in defensive tactics.

Members of the guard were not armed by the unions, since in the given circumstances that would have made them vulnerable to police frame-ups. But many of them had guns of their own at home, which were used to hunt game; and those could quickly have been picked up if needed to fight off an armed attack by Silver Shirt thugs.

At the drill sessions, lectures were given on tactics used in the past by antilabor vigilantes in this country and fascists abroad. Discussions were then held to work out defensive measures to meet attacks of the kind.

An intelligence department was also set up. Its task was to keep a lookout for fascist and anti-Semitic literature and activities, fink propaganda, and the like. One particular episode graphically illustrated the breadth of the intelligence arm, as well as the guard's effectiveness in action. It came about when the Silver Shirts attempted to hold another rally, to be addressed by Pelley himself.

On the day of the scheduled affair a cab driver delivered Pelley to a residence in the city's silk-stocking district. The driver immediately reported this to Rainbolt, who telephoned the place and warned that Pelley would run into trouble if he went ahead. To show he was not bluffing, Rainbolt led a section of the union guard to Calhoun Hall, where the rally was to be held that night. Arrival of the union forces caused the audience to leave in a hurry, and the demagogue never did show up. Then, around midnight, another cab driver called Rainbolt to report that he had just dumped Pelley at the Milwaukee depot in time to catch a night train to Chicago.

Following that incident the Teamsters took a step calculated to throw a further scare into the would-be union busters. It came in the form of a special notice printed on the front page of the *Northwest Organizer* of September 29, 1938. The notice instructed all captains of the defense guard to have their squads up to full strength forthwith and to be prepared to mobilize them, ready for action, on short notice.

The move seemed to have the desired effect, for the Silver Shirts transferred their next meeting to the neighboring city of St. Paul. It was held on October 28 at the Minnehaha Hall, and the place was well guarded by cops. Zachary was the main speaker. As reported in the newspapers the next morning, he boasted:

"Leaders of 544 have said we cannot hold meetings in Minneapolis, but we shall hold them, with the aid of the police. The police know that some day they'll need our support and that's why they're supporting us now."

Zachary's line was taken seriously by the Teamsters for several reasons. More could have been involved in the St. Paul affair than a mere effort to boost the sagging morale of the profascist elements by holding a successful meeting. Part of the scheme could also have been to bring pressure upon the Minneapolis authorities to provide them with comparable police protection in that city as well. If so, Associated Industries was in all likelihood involved in the maneuver.

Acting on such assumptions, the high command of the union defense guard decided to put on a public show of force. The aim was twofold: to make it plain to one and all that the Silver Shirts were not going to operate in Minneapolis without a serious fight and, simultaneously, to test the guard's efficiency in the course of such a demonstration.

Toward those ends an emergency mobilization of the defense formation was called on one hour's notice. Only three people knew what was up. As part of the test all others were left with the impression that a real crisis had developed. By the designated assembly time, just sixty minutes after the first call went out, about 300 members of the guard had turned out ready for action—an impressive performance.

The mobilization took place on a vacant plot of land in the center of the city, so a lot of people would see what was going on. Once the men were assembled there, Rainbolt explained that it had been a practice operation to give yet another warning to the Silver Shirts and their supporters among the employers. A clinical discussion was then held about the results of the test.

Since all kinds of personal plans for the evening had been rudely upset, a bit of entertainment was in order by way of compensation. So the guard was marched in a long column—armbands prominently displayed—to a downtown burlesque theater, where a block of seats had been reserved.

As for the ultrarightists, they appeared to have gotten the union's message loud and clear. Zachary made no further attempts to hold rallies in Minneapolis; fascist propaganda tapered off; and after a time it became evident that the Silver Shirt organizing drive in the city had been discontinued altogether.

Despite this favorable turn in the situation, the union defense guard was maintained as a form of insurance against any resurgence of the fascist threat. But the nature of its activities underwent a change. Target practice and drill sessions were tapered off. Gradually the guard's functions shifted mainly to monitoring union picnics and other large social gatherings. Through occasional public displays of this kind the antilabor forces were reminded of the continued existence of the defense formation.

On balance, Local 544 had not only warded off another capitalist attack. The experience with the Silver Shirts had given many of its members a better understanding of the need for workers' self-defense, and the best militants had gained deeper insight into the laws of class struggle.

2. 50,000 anti-Nazis answer SWP call
1,780 LaGuardia cops protect Nazis from workers wrath in brutal attack on demonstrators

An imposing, fighting demonstration of fifty thousand workers assembled near Madison Square Garden on Monday evening to protest the first big fascist mobilization in New York City.

In addition to the fifty thousand demonstrators who responded to the call of the Socialist Workers party for a labor rally against the fascist concentration, official police estimates given to the press counted another fifty thousand among the spectators. With few exceptions, the latter made clear their sympathy with the aims and slogans of the demonstrating thousands. With a brutality recalling the days of Czarist Cossacks, 1,780 of Mayor La Guardia's police, the largest number of cops ever collected in the city against a single demonstration, slugged and trampled under horses' hooves scores of workers in an unsuccessful attempt to break up the demonstration. From 6 p.m. until 11, the workers engaged in a series of bitter clashes with police. The size of the workers' counterdemonstration far exceeded the expectations of even the most optimistic.

Efforts had been made on all hands, prior to the Nazi meeting, to minimize the significance of the call issued by the Socialist Workers party, to smother it by a campaign of silence, and to sabotage it directly.

Supercilious critics of the "Trotskyists" in the social-democratic camp sought to dispose of the counterdemonstration by ridicule and disdainful talk of our alleged insignificance. Neither the Socialist party of Norman Thomas nor the Social-Democratic Federation would take any cognizance of the call for the demonstration, much less endorse it. They were nowhere to be found in the demonstration.

CP role despicable

The Stalinists played a particularly despicable role, which aroused widespread bewilderment and confusion in their own ranks, which contain thousands of workers who really want to fight against fascism.

On the day of the demonstration, all that the *Daily Worker* had to say was its report of a speech in favor of democracy by acting Mayor Newbold Morris. Not a single word about the "Trotskyists" or their call. It would have been a little embarrassing even to such brazen pen-slaves as Stalin employs in New York to write, on this occasion, diatribes against the "Trotsky-fascists"!

As for the Monday edition of the *Freiheit*, Yiddish organ of the Stalinists, it solved the whole annoying problem by not printing one line about the Nazi demonstration or about the counterdemonstration. It just shoved its head into a deep pile of sand.

The three other Jewish daily papers in New York City—the conservative *Morning Journal*, the "progressive" *Day*, and the social-democratic *Forward*—united in printing virtually the same news stories and editorials, using, in all cases, the same arguments and in many cases even the same words. Instead of a call to the Jewish workers to demonstrate against their sworn enemies, the fascists, they joined hands in a sniveling, cowardly appeal to their readers to do anything in the world Monday evening—go to the movies, stay at home, go to the mountains or the seashore—anything except go to the anti-Nazi demonstration.

Morris' radio appeal

Acting Mayor Newbold Morris issued a special last minute appeal to the population of New York City to stay away from our rally.

"Information has come to me," said this pompous professional democrat, "that some citizens, indignant at tonight's Bund meeting at Madison Square Garden, are planning to be present at or about the Garden entrance to express displeasure. In the interest of public order, I want to urge all citizens having no business at the meeting to remain away from the Garden and its immediate vicinity."

This statement, broadcast on the radio before the meeting and of course prominently featured later

---

Reprinted from the February 22, 1939, issue of the *Socialist Appeal*.

by the *Daily Worker*, was calculated to reduce the demonstration called by the SWP to an insignificant handful of individuals who could be dispersed by the army of cops with a wave of the hand.

Yet, in spite of this imposing array of sabotaging talent from the ranks of the fireside "democrats" whose efforts were supplemented by the repeated emphasis given in the capitalist press to the fact that, as the *World-Telegram* put it, "neither the Socialist party nor the Communist party in this city had announced up to this morning (Monday) any intention to demonstrate or otherwise take cognizance of the meeting," and that "only" the Trotskyists would be there—thousands of New York workers began converging upon Madison Square Garden even before 6 o'clock in the evening, that is, more than two hours before the Nazi meeting was scheduled to open!

It goes without saying that they were not Trotskyists, these thousands who, by 8 o'clock, reached enormous proportions. But their presence around the Garden, in response to the appeal of a comparatively small organization, showed that the Socialist Workers party had correctly gauged the sentiments of the best sections of the New York working class.

Rank and file comes

Rank and file Stalinists, perplexed and irritated by the criminal sabotage of their officialdom, but nevertheless determined to demonstrate "unofficially" against the Nazis, whom they realize to be the menace they are, came to our rally by the thousands.

No less gratifying was the fact that one of the banners borne in the demonstration signified that the youth organization of the Thomasite Socialist party had come to the anti-Nazi rally in spite of the shabby indifference of the party elders.

Equally inspiring was the contingent of Negro workers who came spontaneously to the tumultuous gathering, bearing their own posters and placards, including one signed by the Universal Negro Improvement Association.

Squadrons move on Garden

By 6 p.m. the first organized squadron of members of the Socialist Workers party and Young People's Socialist League (4th International) left from a central assembly point for the Garden area. It was followed in swift succession by three other squadrons—each assigned to a specific concentration point.

Upon their arrival, they found what the *New York Times* subsequently described as a wall of cops, in uniform, in plain clothes and mounted, "who made of Madison Square Garden an almost impregnable fortress to anti-Nazis."

The Garden was blocked off for blocks around in all four directions. Traffic, both vehicular and pedestrian, was detoured in the most elaborate way.

Cops versus workers

Nobody was allowed to penetrate the solid wall of cops who was not in possession of a ticket to the Nazi meeting, purchased in advance. The smallest gathering of workers, even of ordinary passersby, was instantaneously broken up by the cops in order to prevent a concentration.

But in spite of all their efforts, thousands of workers from all parts of greater New York did begin to collect along the streets immediately outside the blocked-off quadrangle—primarily on 48th Street on the south and 51st Street on the north, pressing in both cases towards 8th Avenue, on which the main entrance to the Garden is located.

Thousands cheer SWP

The placards and posters of the Socialist Workers party were uplifted amid the cheers of thousands. Almost simultaneously, on both streets, which by this time were choked to capacity by huge crowds reaching from Broadway to 8th Avenue, a spontaneous drive was launched to get through the police lines and into the immediate Garden area.

Action began on 48th Street. From the corner of 8th Avenue where a solid line of mounted cops was stationed, stirrup to stirrup, they made a furious attack on the assembled demonstrators. Moving in both directions, one group of cops trampled down a throng of patriotic war veterans and cut their American flag to ribbons, while another group smashed brutally into the mass of workers.

Masses reform ranks

Although the Cossacks made repeated sallies into the workers' crowd, the mass formed and reformed, stoutly determined to hold their own until they gathered sufficient strength to exercise their right to assemble and to picket whether the cops granted it or not.

Meanwhile, 51st Street was jammed from Broadway to 8th Avenue with a crowd so densely packed together that it was virtually impassable. Just as close a line of Cossacks stood at the 8th Avenue end, backed by hundreds of police on foot. The forward surge of the workers bent that line over and over again but did not succeed in breaking through.

Defense guards needed

It was evident, especially at this point, that even a large gathering of workers cannot easily attain its objective unless these workers have been organized thoroughly in advance and trained to act in sharp coordination. It was evident, in other words, that for the complete success of such a demonstration a militant, organized Workers Defense Guard is indispensable.

The fury of the workers increased with every minute. They kept shouting angrily at the Cossacks, and booed them for every vicious plunge into the crowd.

"Down with the Nazi terrorists!" they roared the cry of the Socialist Workers party.

"We demand the right to picket!" they shouted.

Surrounded by an unbreakable phalanx, one SWP speaker after another, lifted on the shoulders of huskies, made terse and militant speeches to the workers, who cheered so lustily that they could be heard, literally, for blocks away.

Max Shachtman, editor of the *Socialist Appeal*, was the first to speak. He pointed out that the La Guardia administration, elected to office by the vote of New York labor, was showing an amazing concern over the so-called "democratic rights" of the Nazi assassins to hold a mobilization meeting which was an insult and a provocation to the working people of the city. The same administration, however, which gave such unprecedented police protection to the Fascist gang, was using the police to deprive the workers of *their* democratic rights, notably the right to assemble and to picket—rights supposedly guaranteed by the Constitution and by several decisions of the Federal and Supreme courts.

He warned the workers of New York against being caught asleep in the struggle against Fascism, as was the case in so many countries of Europe. It *can* happen here, he cried, but it will be too late to stop it when the concentration camps are being filled. His appeal for the Workers Defense Guards as protection against fascist assaults, so strikingly underscored by the conduct of New York's "democratic" police, was enthusiastically hailed by the crowd.

Shachtman was followed by other spokesmen of the party. The speakers included James Burnham, Martin Abern, manager of the *New International*, Nathan Gould, National Secretary of the YPSL, B.J. Widick, the party's labor secretary, Bill Morgan, leading militant in the unemployed movement, Richard Ettlinger, prominent among the progressive office workers, Paul G. Stevens, Irving Pankin of the YPSL, and numerous others.

Parade down Broadway

Suddenly, after having stood their ground for three hours, the workers veered around upon the signal of the demonstration's spokesman and marched down the street in a tremendous column for a parade down Broadway.

It is a long time since New York's most famous avenue has seen such a militant, vociferous, determined, and large working-class parade. The police, concentrated around the Garden, were so scattered along Broadway that they did not even attempt to halt the parade.

Shouting their slogans as they marched along the almost equally crowded sidewalks, the paraders, led by the banner-bearers of the Socialist Workers party, turned south from 51st Street and, after reaching 42nd Street with unbroken ranks numbering thousands, moved west to 8th Avenue again. At that point, the marchers turned north and proceeded in the direction of the Garden, which is located between 49th and 50th Streets.

Cops attack

Just as the head of the march reached 47th Street, it ran smack into a newly-formed line of cops. Without a word of warning, they plunged into the parade, mounted cops in the lead, with rows of foot cops behind them. The horses were driven straight into the ranks of the marchers, first in the center of the street and then on the sidewalks. Shop windows were shattered to smithereens, and workers wounded by jagged splinters. Others went down under the horses, as is so graphically revealed by the sensational photographs which were published in the press. Clubs were drawn and swung freely and viciously.

This was not in Czarist Moscow, in Hitler's Berlin or Mussolini's Rome. No! This took place in the domain of "democratic" New York, under the administration of "progressive" Mayor La Guardia, successful candidate of the American Labor Party in the last election!

Notwithstanding the assault, the lines of the march were still reformed. The parade turned down 47th Street and proceeded once more to Broadway. There a fresh attempt was made to organize a meeting at the Duffy Monument. But another police concentration was on hand and a violent struggle ensued.

The workers refused to be shoved around. They had seen many of their comrades seriously injured and beaten. When the police sought to disperse the marchers, they encountered the stiffest resistance.

March terminates

Finally, after breaking through the police line, the crowd drove through to 49th Street, where the march was terminated by an announcement from an SWP speaker whom the police, helplessly trying to break through the firm block of workers, sought in vain to reach so that he could be torn down from the taxicab he had mounted in order to address the marchers.

As the militants disbanded, along about midnight, the Tuesday edition of the *Daily Worker* appeared on the street. Unbelievable as it sounds, while the Stalinist sheet had a report of what went on inside the Garden at the Nazi meeting, it did not even mention the fact that there had been tens of thousands of workers gathered near the Garden in a stormy, anti-Nazi protest meeting! From its report, one would conclude that the Nazis held their mobilization undisturbed by the presence of a single worker. The encouragingly huge protest demonstration, the police brutality, prominently featured by every capitalist newspaper, was deliberately and completely suppressed by the Stalinist paper!

Stalinists sabotaged

But that incredibly stupid device will not save Browder and Co. from giving an accounting to their members as well as the workers in general. Everybody in and around New York knows about the demonstration, who initiated, sponsored, and led it. Everybody knows that the Stalinists sabotaged it from first to last. And thousands, including rank-and-file Stalinists of the party and the Young Communist League, are so disturbed by this policy, so ashamed of it, that they will demand an answer to the question that is being asked on all sides.

Meanwhile, the answer to the bigger question— How to fight Fascism?—was given in thunderous tones by the magnificent demonstration which reached its highest note on the cry: Workers Defense Guards to crush the fascist danger!

3. Should fascists be allowed the right of free speech?
A working-class point of view on the question that was brought to the fore again by the professional democrats when the Nazis mobilized at the Garden.
By Joseph Hansen

It seems that the only point of importance that the professional liberals and democrats could see in the big mobilization of the Nazis at Madison Square Garden last week, was their "right of free speech and assembly."

Mayor LaGuardia kept reiterating emphatically that his attachment to Democracy compelled him to grant the Fascists the right to hold their meet-

Reprinted from the March 3, 1939, issue of *Socialist Appeal*.

WORKERS OF NEW YORK!
Stop the Fascists!

PICKET MADISON SQUARE GARDEN, MON., FEB. 20, 6 P. M.!

The fascists are mobilizing at Madison Square Garden Monday night.

Hitler's German-American Bund gangsters, Pelley's Silver Shirt scum and Coughlin's mob of labor-haters have hurled a brazen challenge at the workers of New York.

Wrapping themselves in the cloak of patriotism and "Americanism", the fascists prepare to spew their anti-labor and anti-Jewish poison throughout New York City.

These gangs have already gone too far. They must be stopped.

What are you going to do to stop this murderous crew?

We must not let this filthy, creeping slime get a foothold in New York.

Gather in front of Madison Square Garden Monday by the thousands!

Be there at 6:00 P. M. sharp!

Let the fascists feel the anger and the might of the working class— Get out and picket!

Don't wait for the concentration camps — Act now!

On to Madison Square Garden Monday Night!

Issued by the
SOCIALIST WORKERS PARTY (Fourth International)
116 University Place, New York City

February 1939: Thousands of copies of this leaflet were issued to the workers of New York calling for a mass demonstration on the streets to protest the Fascist meeting scheduled for February 20, 1939, in Madison Sq. Garden. 50,000 workers rallied to the call.

ing and provide them with extraordinary police protection.

The American Civil Liberties Union rushed into print to insist that the right of free speech be extended to the Hitlerites.

One of the numerous committees of the Jewish bourgeoisie, anxious to demonstrate that it loves fairness above all else, did likewise.

Even the wretched little Jewish anarchist weekly published in New York indignantly reproached the Trotskyists for the lack of sense in "demanding the right of free speech and assembly for oneself and at the same time trying to prevent the freedom of speech of our opponents. . . ."

Freedom for Nazis but not for pickets

Before going further into the consideration of the question of "free speech for Fascists," it is interesting and important to record the fact that all the above-mentioned who showed such touching concern for the "democratic rights" of the Nazis, are entirely unconcerned with the brutal police suppression of the picketing rights of the workers who assembled outside the Garden.

The Mayor simply refused to see a delegation which came to protest against the violence of the police who rode down and slugged the picketers.

The American Civil Liberties Union, apparently exhausted by its noble efforts in behalf of the Nazis, didn't utter a peep about the democratic rights of free speech, assembly and picketing being denied the 50,000 anti-Fascists who came to protest the Nazi rally. Ditto for the Jewish committee.

As for the anarchists *Freie Arbeiter Stimme,* it says not a word about the police assaults, but villainously insinuates that the Terrible Trotskyists were really at fault because, Mr. Police Commissioner, they planned a violent attack on the Nazis who were innocently celebrating Washington's Birthday. Unbelievable, but here are its exact words:

"But there are times when people who endeavor to do social work must reflect ten times, a hundred times, before they come out with an appeal for acts of violence."

What the problem really involves

The question of "democratic rights for the Nazis" cannot be resolved on the basis of liberal phrasemongers. All such a discussion can produce is a bewildering tangle of words and abstractions. At a more decisive stage, as all recent experience has proved, it produces a first class disaster not only for the working class but also for the professional liberals and democrats themselves.

How many of them, indeed, are there in the concentration camps, in prison and in exile who are continuing the thoroughly futile and abstract discussion over whether or not the Fascist gangsters should be granted the "democratic rights of free speech and assembly"!

And what is most decisive—this is the point which leads us directly to a solution of the problem that seems to agitate so many people—is the fact that in Italy, in Germany, in Austria, in Czechoslovakia, in Spain, the democrats were so concerned with preserving the "rights" of the Fascists that they concentrated all their attacks and repressive measures upon those workers and those labor organizations which sought to conduct a militant struggle against the Fascists and for the preservation and extension of their truly democratic rights and institutions.

It is when the bourgeois "democrats" like Giolitti in Italy and Bruening in Germany, had done all in their power to smash the most progressive and active sections of the working class—as LaGuardia and his police tried to do on a smaller scale in New York last week—that the Fascists concluded successfully their march to totalitarian power. Whoever forgets this important lesson from abroad, is a fool. Whoever tries to keep others ignorant of this lesson, is a rogue.

A simple example

Let us take a simple example which every worker has experienced dozens of times.

A strike is called. The authorities promptly jump into the situation in order to protect the "democratic rights" of the scabs and the company gunmen who guard them. The "right to work" of the scab, which is guaranteed by the capitalist government, amounts in reality to his "right" to starve out the striking workers and reduce them to helpless pawns of the employers.

Millions of workers have learned the futility and deceptiveness of the academic discussion of the scab's "democratic rights," as well as of appealing to the government and its police to "arbitrate" the dispute involved. They try to solve the question, as they must, *in the course of struggle.* The workers throw their picket-lines around the struck plant. The conflict between the scab's "right" to break a strike and the workers' right to live, is also *settled* in the course of struggle—in favor of those who plan better, organize better, and fight better.

Same rule applies on broader scene

The same rule applies in the struggle against the much bigger scab movement that Fascism represents.

The workers who spend all their time and energy in the abstract discussion of the Nazi's "democratic rights"—to say nothing of working themselves into a lather in defense of these "rights"—will end their discussion under a Fascist club in a concentration camp.

The workers who delude themselves and waste their time begging the capitalist democrats in office to "act" against the Fascists, will end up in the same place, just as the workers of Italy, Germany, and Austria did.

The workers have more vital concerns. They are and should be interested in defending and expanding their democratic rights. But not in any abstract sense. These rights are the concrete rights of free speech, assembly, press, the right to organize, strike, and picket, without which an independent working class simply cannot exist.

A decaying capitalism—of which Fascism is only a natural product—seeks constantly to restrict and destroy these rights, which are not truly genuine even in "normal" times. These rights can only be defended from the assaults of capitalism and its ugly offspring, Fascism, in the same way in which they were first acquired: by the tireless, aggressive, unbending, independent struggle of the working class.

The wailing and weeping about the Nazi's "rights" can safely be left to the prissy liberals and the phony democrats.

The self-preservation of the working class demands that it cut through all abstract chatter and smash the Fascist gangs by decisive and relentless action.

4. Comrade Cross invents a problem (excerpt)
By Felix Morrow

I have carefully read and reread Comrade Cross' article, "The Relationship Between Free Speech and the Proletarian Revolution" [see the same number of the *Bulletin*]. I regret that it is not a fruitful contribution to analyzing the new problems concretely raised by the slogan of Workers Defense Guards. That slogan does raise important new problems. Comrade Cross has, however, simply invented a nonexistent problem; he has done so, as I shall show, in order to propagate an historical interpretation of the Thermidorean reaction in Soviet Russia which is alien to the Trotskyist explanation of the degeneration of the workers state in Russia. The free speech "problem" invented by him serves merely as a springboard for a false

Reprinted from SWP *Internal Bulletin* No. 8, May 1939.

historical theory. Comrade Cross is within his rights in raising any and all questions during the preconvention discussion. But the main body of his article is an argument against a straw man, for it is *not* true that the party "denies free speech to fascists"; while the real logical motivation of his article—the enunciation of an anti-Trotskyist explanation of the degeneration of the proletarian dictatorship in Russia—is simply asserted without a word of argument or proof.

Comrade Cross writes: "The current articles in the press of the SWP have unambiguously pledged that party to most violent action in smashing the fascists and in denying them the right to speak. A more thoughtful leadership would simply agitate to smash the fascists, and leave the question of their right to speak alone. The arguments used are: that the avowed object of the fascists is to smash all democratic rights. They would deny us the right to speak, put us in concentration camps and shoot us. Consequently, why should they be allowed free speech?"

Where did Comrade Cross find the *Socialist Appeal* saying that fascists should not be allowed to speak? He cites no issues and pages of the *Appeal*—and with good reason, for he could find no such citations. Yet he blandly reports the *Appeal*'s arguments for this nonexistent position.

A very fruitful discussion can be had on the extremely delicate problems connected with calling upon the workers to fight against the fascists: when to speak purely in defensive terms, and when to go over to terms indicating an offensive against the fascists. For the moment, it is clear, political realities—the speedy growth of the fascists, our own weakness—dictate defensive terms. A warning must also be given to the party against a too-technical conception of the formation of Workers Defense Guards: unless the Guards are merely the first ranks, carrying with them nonparty and nonguard elements in their actions, we shall find ourselves defeating the real purpose for mobilizing the guards: getting the masses to move with us. We must also convince the party membership—and above all the youth—that the guard is a practical, feasible, and pressing task. These and other problems deserve discussion. But not this invention of Comrade Cross.

It has long been clearly thought out, in the Bolshevik movement, where we stand on the question of free speech. First of all, "free speech" belongs to the category of "civil liberties." Let those who will, engage in this activity—we certainly don't denounce the *existence* of the American Civil Liberties Union—but the task of the revolutionist and of the working class and its allies is the fight for the *democratic rights of the working class.*

From the concept of "civil liberties," the American Civil Liberties Union logically arrives at the point of offering its services to fascists who in isolated instances run afoul of a progressive mayor or police chief. What do we say about such actions of the ACLU? We say: for every fascist persecuted by the state, ten thousand workers are persecuted. We are ready to tell the ACLU of more cases of workers' rights being violated than the ACLU can possibly handle. The ACLU knows this as well as we. But the ACLU is so anxious to prove its respectability, so fawningly worried about the good opinion of bosses and their stooges, that the ACLU takes good money and lawyers that might be used to help persecuted workers, and diverts it to the use of the fascists.

This concrete criticism of the ACLU does not involve a denial of free speech to the fascists. Moreover, is it our business to tell the capitalist state what to do about the fascists, to please give them free speech? Not at all. We give advice only to the workers, and we call upon them to fight fascism. The only point at which we will suppress the free speech of the fascists is only in the broad sense that, in carrying out the seizure of state power, we shall undoubtedly have to smash the fascist organizations and suppress the fascist cadres.

5. Resolution of July 1939 convention on workers defense guard

1. The collapse of the New Deal, and the insuperable, ever-mounting internal conflicts of United States capitalism are beginning to pose more and more directly to the U.S. bourgeoisie the necessity for abandoning parliamentary democracy and resorting to fascism as the sole means for preserving its power and privilege; and these same factors simultaneously open the minds of large numbers among the unemployed, farmers, middle classes and demoralized proletarians to fascist demagogy and organization.

2. Recent months have witnessed a profound

Reprinted from the July 7, 1939, issue of *Socialist Appeal.*

transformation in the character of the fascist movement in the United States. Before this, it had been confined largely to individual cranks, eccentrics, and dilettante intellectuals, and "foreign" groups such as the various Italian fascist societies and the Nazi Bund. Now, for the first time, it is becoming a serious, native, mass movement. In the first stage of this transformation, the Coughlinites in the big cities, and to a lesser extent the Silver Shirts in the farming areas and smaller towns, are playing a major role. Whatever may be the eventual fate of these two particular groups, and whatever may be the episodic rises and declines of the fascist movement as a whole, it is certain to grow in extent and depth until its sources have been rooted out. This can be accomplished by nothing short of the social revolution.

Immediate problem

3. The transformation of the fascist movement dictates the transformation of the methods of defense against it. Theoretical analysis and abstract propaganda, to which specifically antifascist activities had to be more or less confined so long as fascism in this country remained primarily a threat for the future, become altogether inadequate when fascism has become a reality of the present.

4. The long-term defense against fascism can be only the achievement of the social revolution. Meanwhile, however, there is the immediate and direct problem of the physical defense of the organization, lives, and liberties of the workers, which the fascists aim first to weaken and then to destroy, from the physical assaults of the fascist gangs. The experience of all countries, including the United States, proves beyond any doubt whatever that the agencies of the bourgeois-democratic state will not and cannot carry out this defense; but that on the contrary, reliance upon these agencies guarantees the smashing of the workers and the victory of the fascists. Only the workers themselves, relying on their own means and strength, can defend their own organizations and life and liberties. The only possible form of defense against the fascists is the Workers Defense Guard. Whereas, formerly, the Workers Defense Guard has been primarily a slogan for agitation, the point has now been reached, and more than reached when the concrete task of the actual building of the Workers Defense Guard must begin in action.

5. The Workers Defense Guard is, from one point of view, an outgrowth and development of the picket squads used by virtually all unions in strikes. From the beginning, however, the Defense Guard differs in key respects from the picket squad. The Guard is permanent, whereas the picket squads are usually created only for the duration of the strike. The duties of the Guard are not merely picketing, defense against scabs, etc., but at all times the defense of the headquarters and rights of the union and its members. Moreover, the tasks of the Guard must be conceived, from the start, not in narrow terms of the given single union which may be first involved, but of the labor movement as a whole, and indeed of all groups, individuals, organizations, racial minorities, etc., threatened or attacked by the fascists, vigilantes or other reactionaries. The duty of the Guard is to defend all who need defense from the assaults of the fascists. To carry out this duty, the Guard must be trained and disciplined, and function democratically as an autonomous body. From a second point of view, the Workers Defense Guard is the preparation for the far broader organization of the masses, with far greater tasks, which will in the future have the task of defending the masses against the counterrevolution.

Enlisting the unions

6. From the nature of the Workers Defense Guard and its tasks, it follows that the Guard should take form wherever possible through the established unions. Revolutionists within the unions must attempt to win the union members as a whole to a realization of the necessity of the Guard and must aim to have the unions initiate the actual building of the Guard. Where a union forms units of the Guard, the aim must be from the beginning to extend the scope and base of the Guard beyond the normal confines of union organization and activity; by drawing into the Guard unemployed, youth, and others who are not members of the union (and in many cases are not in a position to be members of any union), by linking up with other unions in the building of the Guard, by establishing relations with the Guard in other cities and by amplifying the types of activities undertaken by the Guard.

7. In localities where it is at present impossible to enlist the established unions in the task of building the Guard, it is now necessary, in addition to constant agitation for union initiative, to take concrete steps in the formation of the Guard with what forces are available. Where such forces are meager it would be an error to regard the group that can be formed as a Workers Defense Guard in the full sense; rather, since the genuine Guard can be built only by enlisting the masses, are such groups skeletons or embryos of the Guard. They cannot substitute their action for that of the masses, but must aim to win the masses especially in the trade unions to the task of building the Guard, by adding on however a modest scale, the lesson of action and example to that of agitation. In New York City, Newark, and elsewhere, first steps have been taken along these lines by the formation of the Anti-Fascist Labor Guard.

United front action

8. The struggle against fascism makes possible, and demands, the broadest possible united front. The essential requirements for membership in the defense Guard must be formulated simply as a willingness to fight the fascists, to defend labor and other organizations and groups from the fascist and vigilante attacks, and to accept the democratic discipline of the Guard. While taking every precaution to make sure of the integrity of every applicant and to preserve the Guard from provocateurs, stool-pigeons, and irresponsible or light-minded elements, the effort must be made to enlist membership and support as broadly and widely as possible on this basis.

9. The significance of our party's advocacy and support of the Guard is in no way limited to the specific and all-important tasks which the Guard can and must fulfill. Advocacy and support of the Guard is an integral and decisive part of the political program of our party and a political weapon of the utmost importance. Experience has already shown, and will more fully confirm in the future, that the slogan of building the Guard meets with an immediate response from the best sections of the workers and the youth, and concretizes the whole meaning of our conception of the struggle against fascism in a manner accomplished by no other part of our program.

Supplementary motions

1. The convention instructs the incoming National Committee to appoint a special commission to be in charge of carrying out and coordinating on a national scale, the work of the Party in connection with the building of the Workers Defense Guard.

6. Proposals on initiating defense guards

The following suggestions on organizing defense guards were attached to the SWP Political Committee minutes of July 25, 1939, and were distributed to all party branches. They deal with efforts to initiate defense guards by the party in situations where the trade union leaders were unwilling to take the lead in defending workers against fascist attacks. Implementation of these proposals was forestalled by the outbreak of the war.

(1) The general line of the Workers Defense Guard is laid down by our convention resolution which makes clear that we attempt to help in building a mass guard based upon the support of trade unions and other mass organizations.

(2) The convention resolution also makes clear that we do not merely agitate and carry on literary propaganda for this idea, while waiting for the unions to take the lead in establishing the guard, but that at every available opportunity we utilize our available forces to set up nuclei of the future mass guard.

(3) It is obvious that at the present time in New York no unions or other mass organizations are ready to initiate and support the organization of a labor defense guard. These objective conditions

dictate to us that we establish, as the immediate policy, a specialized type of activity in order to reach our objective by a flank movement as it were.

(4) The New York guard will select two favorable neighborhoods; one in the Bronx district, the other near the Flatbush district, and will "dig" themselves into these neighborhoods in the following manner:

(a) They will hold regular open air meetings under the auspices of the guard.

(b) They will seek to establish relations with every single available trade unionist and contact in the neighborhood with the view of eventually establishing relations with every single local union of the neighborhood.

(5) A speakers bureau will be organized in an attempt to send special representatives of the guard to address the organizations above mentioned.

(6) The guard will sponsor model resolutions which they will attempt to have their contacts and friends introduce in these organizations.

(7) The guard will organize as one of its central activities a well-planned and coordinated espionage system for the following purposes:

(a) to gain full knowledge of the scope, character, and implications of all the groups adhering to the Coughlin movement, the Christian Front, and the other fascist groups.

(b) To have full and accurate knowledge of all of the plans, moves and preparations of the enemy camp.

(8) With the ground well prepared by this deliberate day-to-day work of establishing connections with union members, local union organizations, fraternal bodies, etc., and with the full knowledge of the ramifications of the enemy organizations, gained by the most painstaking efforts, the guard will be in a position to make a great drive to secure finances from numerous Jewish storekeepers and other sympathetic individuals, etc., to carry on its activities and counteract the propaganda of the Christian Mobilizers and the other fascists to "Buy Christian and boycott Jewish business!" etc., etc.

(9) Using its knowledge of the plans of the enemy, the guard will attempt to contact the organizations in its neighborhood, with whom it presumably has established close fraternal connections, in order to gain the support of these organizations for *mass actions* in defense of the democratic rights of labor, etc., to be conducted against the Coughlinites. The guard becomes thus not only an organization of propaganda and agitation, but also an organization of *action*. It must be understood, however, that we always carry on our actions on the basis of our ability to mobilize larger masses behind our aims and moves than simply the members of the guard nucleus or even of the party membership.

(10) The guard will make preparations to publish a magazine to be written in a vivid and attractive style emphasizing the nature of the guard organization as one of action and aggressive opposition to the fascist movement.

(11) Given the present numerical strength, the guard will dress in uniform only in inside meetings. A small band of uniformed men marching in the streets tends at the present time to antagonize and alienate people, rather than aiding the guard in its basic purpose of winning support for itself of larger strata of the population.

(12) The guard is to emphasize its non-political character in all of its agitation and propaganda, and to stress that it is not a "subversive" organization, but is an organization protecting the democratic rights of the labor movement against the challenge of fascist dictatorship.

(13) The guard is to carry on all of its present propaganda under defensive slogans, always *protecting* the rights of the workers, *defending* meetings from unjust provocation or attack, etc.

(14) The guard is to be governed in its organization and practical work by a council with one coordinating officer, the organizer.

7. Coughlin delivers fascist blast against workers defense guards
By Joseph Hansen

In a violent one-hour tirade last Sunday over his nationwide radio hookup, Father Coughlin attacked the formation of antifascist union guards, as if he feared that any minute they might mop up the fascist gangs he is organizing.

Father Coughlin's attack was specifically directed against Harry Milton's proposal to Local 66 of the International Ladies Garment Workers Union that they organize Antifascist Union Guards. Coughlin's attack on Milton should dispel the last doubt which might linger in anyone's mind that Father Coughlin is deliberately planning to introduce fascism in America.

This attack proves once and for all that Father Coughlin realizes perfectly that antifascist union guards are the ONE FORCE which can stop him cold.

Father Coughlin began his bitter and slanderous attack against the formation of antifascist union guards by reading over the air a resolution which had been introduced in Local 66 of the ILGWU by one of its prominent members, Harry Milton.

Union guard resolution

The resolution urges the ILGWU immediately to organize an antifascist union guard in order to defend itself from fascist groups and preserve the democratic rights and civil liberties of labor.

The resolution is now under consideration by the International Executive Board of the ILGWU.

Father Coughlin slandered Harry Milton throughout his entire period on the air, asserting that Milton "marched against the people of Spain" under the domination of the Stalinists.

Milton's actual record

Harry Milton served with the Independent Labour Party contingent of the 29th Division of the Loyalist Army, heroically defending on the battlefields the Spanish workers against the attack of General Franco's fascist legions. Milton was arrested by the GPU Stalinist secret service—and imprisoned with hundreds of his fellow militiamen, anarchists, socialists, and other militants. Only by the narrowest of margins did he escape death at the hands of Stalin's GPU.

In introducing the resolution in Local 66 of the ILGWU which was attacked by Coughlin, Milton stated:

> "We must not wait until our own union is broken into and smashed by fascist gangs, as they will attempt tomorrow or the day after, but to stop the fascists now, wherever they attempt to deprive any workers or workers' organization of its constitutional rights.
>
> "The Coughlin gangsters have already broken into a workers' headquarters—the Debs School—and have succeeded in breaking up numerous meetings of labor organizations in the city. Last week they tried to break up an American Labor Party meeting where Michael Quill, president of the Transport Workers Union, was the speaker. Fortunately, the transport workers were prepared."

A few weeks ago beside the above-mentioned attacks against labor, the Coughlinites knifed a school teacher on 14th Street in New York City and attempted to break into the headquarters of the Socialist Workers Party, knifing an antifascist who was on guard.

Father Coughlin fears the formation of antifascist labor guards more than any other single force which might attempt to stop him in his plans to thug his way to fascist power in America.

> "Only one thing could have broken our movement—if the adversary had understood its principle and from the first day had smashed, with the most extreme brutality, the nucleus of our movement."
> Hitler

Reprinted from the July 14, 1939, issue of *Socialist Appeal*.

"If the enemy had known how weak we were, it would probably have smashed us to jelly. . . . It would have crushed in blood the very beginning of our work."
—Goebbels

Coughlin understands that the formation of antifascist union guards will prevent him from introducing fascism in America!

That is why he opposes the formation of antifascist union guards with such a deadly fear.

II. STRUGGLES AGAINST FASCISM AT THE END OF WORLD WAR II

The conclusion of the war saw a revival of fascist activity, along with a revival of labor militancy. Counting on an economic downturn to put wind in their sails, the fascists offered their services to big business as a combat force against a new labor upsurge.

The most active of the fascist leaders was Gerald L.K. Smith. Smith began in Louisiana as an aide to Huey Long and an organizer of his "Share the Wealth" movement. After Long's assassination, Smith lost a fight to take control of Long's machine. Shortly thereafter, Smith emerged as a fascist demagogue. In 1942 he formed the Christian National Front and began to publish *The Cross and the Flag*.

In 1945, he began an energetic effort to build a mass base through national tours. His meetings were met with mass protests in Detroit, Minneapolis, Los Angeles, and other cities. These were often initiated by the SWP. The biggest anti-fascist actions occurred in Los Angeles which Smith tried to establish as a major base.

"Report on the Los Angeles Antifascist Campaign," by Murry Weiss details the tactics used by the SWP in encouraging and building a united front that built a mass meeting of 17,000 against Smith on June 21, 1945. Similar tactics brought a further success on October 18 when 20,000 picketed a Smith meeting. This brought Smith's large-scale efforts in Los Angeles to an end.

An article from the August 31, 1945 issue of the *Militant* and the comments by Vincent R. Dunne on this action describe the setback Smith experienced in Minneapolis.

While Smith's star went into decline, other fascist forces began to emerge out of the government apparatus and the two-party system. The leader of this incipient fascist tendency was Senator Joseph R. McCarthy of Wisconsin. Smith played an active role in supporting McCarthy in the next period. Today, Smith retains a tiny following, primarily in the South.

1. Report on the Los Angeles antifascist campaign (abridged)
By Murry Weiss

The first stage of the antifascist campaign launched by the Los Angeles Local on June 21st has been concluded. Now it is necessary to sum up a body of extraordinarily valuable experience. This experience is all the more precious in view of the inevitable development of the struggle against fascism on a broader scale in the period that lies immediately ahead.

American fascists, such as Gerald L.K. Smith, are already busy preparing for large-scale operations. They scurry up and down the country seeking concentration points. Their natural arena are the large population-swollen industrial centers such as Detroit and Los Angeles where monopoly capital is harried by present and future "labor troubles." In these areas they try to build a mass base among the dislocated and discontented middle-class; the old-age pension movement, veterans groups, religious sects, etc.

In our analysis of the Smith movement, we must avoid exaggerations. To overestimate Smith's present strength or to exaggerate his ties with big business in Southern California is in some respects as dangerous as the softheaded evalua-

From SWP *Discussion Bulletin*, Vol. VII, No. 8, August 1945.

tion of Smith as a lunatic and an "inconsequential rabble-rouser."

G.L.K. Smith, a typical product of the pioneer American fascist movements, came to Los Angeles to persuade big business in Southern California that he could be useful to them in settling accounts with the labor movement. For this purpose he had to show strength, dynamic abilities, a large movement. Has he succeeded in doing this? No doubt powerful elements among the rich farmers and capitalists toy with the idea of utilizing Smith. But it is obvious that Smith has not yet been given the go-ahead signal and the necessary finances to accomplish his purpose. Our analysis of Smith's campaign and his tactics must proceed from this premise—he seeks to make a show of strength. He seeks to impress the big powers with his potentialities as an organizer of anti-union combat forces and with his skill in manipulating race antagonisms and provoking race riots.

The ranks of labor in Los Angeles are swollen with new recruits from the deep South, both Negro and white. Large masses of reactionary middle-class elements are mobilized in and around Los Angeles by the very process of the war. The zoot suit riots, carefully studied by the fascists, gave an indication of how soldiers and sailors could be incited against racial minorities and how a pogrom atmosphere can be created in an American city. Smith's activities constitute a mortal threat to the working class. This was and remains our starting point. Smith's movement is not the isolated German-American Bund, wearing stormtroopers' uniforms and meeting in the Deutsches-Haus. He moves behind a heavy defensive covering of "Christians Unite" and "Against Fascism and Communism!" He works through the churches, the old age pension movement, and every other possible defensive camouflage. Thus when we formulated the policy of our antifascist campaign, our central thought was to force the organized working class into consciousness of who Smith was and the necessity of fighting him. In the first period this was the main need.

The line of the campaign was to mobilize the organized forces of the working class for a struggle against Smith. We reasoned: Smith is here to build a mass movement; to win financial support from influential capitalists; to organize combat groups; to unite all reactionary forces under a single banner; to explode the tinder box of racial tension into riots and pogroms; to turn it all into an attack on the labor movement and on the unemployed who tomorrow will struggle for jobs and security. But Smith is only in the initial stage of his campaign. Therefore, we must not allow him to gain time and a foothold but we must smash back with *great power and boldness, with overwhelming preponderance of force.* This was the objective need. This was the message our party would bring to the workers organizations.

When the Section Executive Committee first opened the discussion on our tactics in the struggle against Smith, the leaders of most sections of the labor movement were completely passive to the fascist threat. Others were following a feeble and cowardly policy. In the Stalinist movement and its periphery a great deal of pressure to "do something" against Smith was to be observed. The Jewish organizations were feeling the pressure of the alarmed and apprehensive masses of worker and middle-class Jews.

The policy of those labor leaders who showed at least an awareness of Smith (the Stalinists and the Jewish leaders) contained two main elements. One was what has since been termed the "hush-hush" policy: "Smith is a lunatic crackpot; ignore him, leave him alone and he'll kill himself." When the rising tide of pressure from the militant workers, the Jewish people and other racial minority groups became sufficiently acute, the Stalinists and the Jewish leaders developed the second element of their policy: "Pressure on the existing law-enforcement agencies and auditorium owners." A large scale telephone and letter-writing campaign was organized. Auditorium owners were petitioned to refuse Smith access to their halls. At one point an "anti-lunatic-fringe" committee was formed with a few prominent Stalinist trade unionists at the head. This Committee died still-born and is interesting only as a symptom of the policy that was being followed.

With each successful meeting of Smith, hammer blows were struck at the policy of "hush-hush." Cowardly silence and petitions to auditorium owners proved their ineffectiveness. More and more workers were being drawn into the movement for antifascist *action*. We learned later of pressure being applied by various militant CIO unionists.

It is on this background that the Section Executive Committee considered the campaign and worked out policy.

At the meeting of the SEC on June 21st, the discussion at first revolved around the question: Shall we picket Smith's Philharmonic meeting of June 25th? We had a proposal from the Shachtmanites for a united front picket demonstration on the 25th. The proposal of the Shachtmanites served one purpose. It forced us to seriously consider the whole question of the fight against Smith—something we had not done previously. As the debate on this question developed, it became clear to all the comrades that a much broader question was involved: the need for an energetic long-term campaign against Smith was agreed upon; the main tactical orientation of propelling the labor movement into action was also agreed on.

The letter from the WP [Workers Party—the organization Shachtman formed after he split from the SWP in 1940] was addressed to the Socialist Party, Socialist Labor Party, Industrial Workers of the World, and the Socialist Workers Party. Their proposal stemmed from the main line they followed throughout the campaign. Draper expressed it clearly when he told us, "We expect nothing from the labor movement at this time in the struggle against the fascists. It is up to the socialists to act." All the SEC members, including the comrades who favored a picket line, appraised the policy of the Shachtmanites as sterile and adventuristic. If it is true that Smith is a fascist bent on destroying the labor movement, then obviously what is needed is a resolute and persistent campaign to organize the united front of all the powerful workers' organizations. This is the force that will crush fascism! How can a serious revolutionary policy fail to orient from the basic consideration of a united front tactic towards the Stalinist organizations? Why did the Shachtmanites appeal to the SLP for a united front and to the CPA (Communist Political Association)? Why did they fail completely to see the need for a united front campaign in the labor movement? It will be seen in the future development of the events how the Shachtmanites miscalculated the entire situation ("we expect nothing from the labor movement at this time"), based themselves primarily on a heckling attack on us, *provided comfort to the fascists*, and were overwhelmed by the real course of events.

Comrades Weiss and Tanner were absent from the June 21st SEC meeting because of illness. They proposed in a memorandum to the Committee "the Los Angeles Local should immediately open an anti-fascist campaign" and outlined a proposed plan of attack. The Committee adopted the proposal for the campaign as a whole; dividing on the question of the tactic for June 25th Smith meeting, a majority in favor of the tactic proposed in the Weiss-Tanner document.

We launch the campaign

The comrades of the Section Executive Committee were fully aware of the pressure the Shachtmanites would attempt to exert on the party when we adopted our policy. If we had considered the question from the point of view of factional pluses and minuses, of "getting the best" of the Shachtmanites in a petty sense, we would have gone out and picketed. This would have facilitated our work of getting next to a few workers the Shachtmanites had recruited and were carefully hiding from us. The Shachtmanites put on a campaign of pressure. At two Sunday night lectures on Stalinism conducted by our party, their leading speakers took the floor and presented their policy; called for party members to participate with them in the picket line. At our anti-fascist mass meeting at which we presented our program for the struggle against Smith, three Shachtmanite speakers dominated the discussion period.

The congenital Abernite, Max Sterling, presented himself to a group of our youth as a "raw worker" undecided between us and the Shachtmanites, but inclining towards them because of their militant position on the antifascist struggle. In a word, they threw everything they had into a campaign to shake the party. We anticipated this and took it into the bargain. We had confidence that the correctness of our line would be confirmed. Our new members and our workers cadre would learn from the firsthand experience with Shachtmanism, with the petty-bourgeois adventurers in action.

We can state with absolute certainty that as regards this aspect of the question, that is, the Shachtmanite "offensive", it netted them exactly zero in influence or gains in our ranks. On the other side of the ledger, we succeeded in inoculating the relatively new party members against the old Shachtmanite virus and in developing contact with a few workers who had accidentally joined the WP.

We opened the campaign with a whole series of record moves. We sent telegrams to all labor bodies, racial minority groups, the Communist Political Association, etc. Naturally we had no illusions that this would bring results in and of itself, but it provided the basis for the effective agitational campaign we developed during the following weeks.

We struck out along three main lines. Within the framework of the general united front tactic we developed a special united front maneuver towards the Stalinists. We regarded the Stalinist movement as the key to the situation. The Stalinists control the apparatus of the CIO; the Stalinists have a large Jewish following; there was considerable sentiment in the Stalinist ranks for "action"; and finally, the Stalinist ranks were in the midst of the crisis of their turn [the expulsion of Browder] manifesting a greater susceptibility to our ideas than we have witnessed in many years. We decided to place as much power as we could behind the united front campaign directed towards the Stalinists. The evidence shows that we were very successful in driving our appeal for the united front deep into the ranks of the Stalinist movement. Our open letter was distributed widely at Stalinist mass meetings, at the Hollywood Citizens Committee meeting, at the CIO Council and in the garment center. It was mailed to our contact list as information.

Most important of all, it was a weapon for our comrades in the shops and unions. The open letter became the occasion for an approach to Stalinist shopmates. Even a number of leading Stalinist workers, members of the Section Committee of the CPA, were contacted in this way and made favorable comments. In one case, our comrade presented the open letter to a Stalinist worker in the shop, a die-hard anti-Trotskyist, who declared he was convinced we were right on this point. He then showed the open letter to two other Stalinist workers in the shop, one of whom asserted that the Trotskyists were "certainly sincere in their struggle against fascism." Among the militants in the CIO and in leading Negro circles our united front tactic towards the Stalinists made a good impression. When we observe how our campaign, our tactics and slogans are being carried into the factories, we can mark it down as a new stage of our development. Here, in the shops, we have the greatest testing ground for our slogans, and here is where we are strongest.

The second line of action was the presentation of resolutions in the unions. We started modestly, but quickly realized the extent of possibilities and tried to step up the introduction of resolutions and the content of the resolutions accordingly. At each union meeting we observed that the temper of the workers was relatively hot on this question. The ease with which our resolutions passed prompted us to work on the idea of proposing that one union body, for example, the Auto Council, shall take the initiative in calling for the formation of a Trade Union Committee to combat Smith. We envisaged this as the next step in making the united front a reality. We are convinced that this would have been entirely possible and a trade union committee would have taken shape "from below," so to speak, i.e., from the action of various local unions in meeting together.

In the meantime, however, the accumulated pressure from a number of different directions, ours not least of all, had forced the Stalinists into a more serious move. The fascists planned to hold a mass meeting at the Shrine Auditorium on July 20th. It was clear that all of the previous efforts of the official leaders to stop Smith had fizzled. The pressure of the workers had also forced the AFL and Railroad Brotherhoods tops into stirring. The united front took shape "from above." Our tactics in the resolutions campaign were accordingly adjusted to this new situation, and we shifted over to resolutions endorsing the united front and calling for support to the united front mass meeting, a counterdemonstration to the Smith Shrine meeting, at the Olympic Auditorium on July 20th.

Although the full effectiveness of our resolutions campaign cannot be measured by the list of unions in which we passed resolutions, the score is nevertheless impressive. In all cases the unions forwarded the resolutions to other unions with a "snowballing" effect. Through the direct initiative of the party, we passed resolutions characterizing Smith, condemning him and calling for militant united labor action against him, in the following unions: Marine Fireman's Union; the Consolidated Steel Local of the USWA; the Joint Board of the ILGWU; the United Auto Council, UAW-CIO; Local 9 of the Shipyard Workers Union-CIO (the largest CIO union on the West Coast); an IAM Local at Lockheed Aircraft; and the San Pedro Longshoreman's Union. In a number of other unions resolutions were slated to go through, but further developments made them unnecessary. The key character of the union bodies listed will show why we can realistically state that our resolutions campaign played an important role in mobilizing sentiment for action, putting pressure on the bureaucrats and in developing the antifascist united front of the Los Angeles labor movement.

The third main line of our campaign was work among the racial and national minorities organizations. We very quickly utilized our excellent relations with the Negro press to publicize the party's campaign and its united front slogans. Three of the local Negro newspapers published our press releases. In our discussions with the editors of the Negro press and various Negro worker leaders, our policy was warmly received and approved. The Sunday before the Olympic Auditorium demonstration the party mobilized forces to go into the Negro neighborhood and the Negro churches. Our comrade spoke before 1200 Negro youth in a large church.

Our contact with Jewish organizations has been fruitful in at least one instance. Mr. Gatch, the editor of the *California Jewish Voice*, has taken a militant position on the struggle against Smith. Before the news of the United Front Olympic Auditorium demonstration was announced, he proposed in a lead article that 10,000 antifascists picket the Shrine meeting. Smith has printed photostatic copies of this article as evidence of the violent Jewish plot against him and his "Christians Unite" campaign. Our relations with this editor and a number of other Jewish organizations around him promise to develop into a bloc within the united front.

Recently it has come to light that fascist vigilante elements are organizing, in the agricultural valleys, rifle clubs with anti-Semitic slogans. Gatch has indicated that he is planning to demand from the authorities decisive action against this ominous move, and if immediate action is not forthcoming, he will call for the formation of Jewish youth "Health" clubs. There are other small signs that such sentiment is developing among the Jewish, Mexican, and Negro population. We will of course be in the forefront in raising the slogan of Defense Guards. In every case we will try to deepen the effect of the slogan by linking it to such concrete events or threats as the valley rifle clubs. If the *Jewish Voice* calls for the formation of Jewish Youth clubs for defense, we will advocate joint Jewish, Mexican, Negro, youth, and workers' defense groups.

Two Smith meetings

The Smith meetings at the Philharmonic auditorium on June 25th, and at the Ham'n'Eggers Hall on June 28th were organized on an ostensibly closed basis, admittance by invitation only. Both were overflow meetings of thousands of people. The Shachtmanites called for mass picketing at both meetings. They issued leaflets and conducted a publicity campaign. In our opinion, separate and apart from the question of whether the SWP should have called a picket demonstration, the Shachtmanites' picket demonstrations were puny and ineffective. At the Philharmonic Auditorium, they mobilized *from the street* a hundred and fifty people. Very few of these came down in response to the call, but were obviously antifascist passersby who joined in the picket line for a short time.

Can this demonstration, which was called to "stop the fascists," be considered effective? Can it be compared with the Madison Square Garden demonstration or Los Angeles antifascist demonstrations of 1938? When the party called the workers to demonstrate against the fascists at the Deutsches Haus in Los Angeles in 1938, we had 2,000 workers outside to a few hundred frightened fascists inside. We had unions and factories represented officially in the demonstration, speaking over our sound-truck loudspeaker. We held siege on the fascist meeting so that they didn't dare leave the meeting till long after midnight. Many of them were then severely beaten by Mexican workers from the Dura Steel factory, who had been called out to demonstrate by the party. In New York comrades know what a mass outpouring of working-class strength there was in response to our call.

If there remains a shadow of doubt over the estimate of the Shachtmanite tactic, this is eliminated when we examine the results of their picket line three days later! Here the Smith meeting was conducted in an off street with very few passersby. The real drawing power of the Shachtmanites and a test of the mood of the workers, their willingness to respond to a call from a small organization, could be observed more accurately. Instead of maintaining their 100 to 150 pickets, the second picket line dropped to from twenty-five to fifty according to the most generous estimates!

At both meetings Smith made great capital out of the feeble showing of the Shachtmanites. "We are thousands and they are 25 or 50 at the most, and they talk of breaking up our meeting. If we went out and said 'boo' they'd run. Even the left-wing CIO is not represented out there." In general, he employed the occasion to raise the morale of his meetings, to picture his movement as unconquerable and the opposition as disorganized and feeble.

The Shachtmanites, however, proclaimed these demonstrations as "victories". How a "Picket Smith's Meetings" movement which records a sharp decline from its first to its second action, can be depicted as a victory is very hard to grasp. Overflow fascist meetings are successfully held. They aren't to the slightest extent shaken from enthusiasm and confidence but, on the contrary, draw strength from observing that instead of a mass demonstration of workers' strength, a small handful of "radicals" parade before their meeting. This can be proclaimed an antifascist victory only by irresponsible braggarts who are deaf, dumb, and blind to the teachings of Bolshevik tactics.

Shortly after their second picket demonstration, the Shachtmanites again proposed to meet with us to discuss joint activity in the struggle against Smith. Our Section Executive Committee decided to authorize the organizer to meet with them. In accordance with our traditional policy we were ready to act jointly with any group or individual in the labor movement. We were ready to bloc with them on any question of action that could be commonly agreed upon. We didn't think there were many such actions but we were ready to listen to any proposals. We met with the Shachtmanites, and they presented a united front proposal in a number of variations.

A. That the SWP and the WP and perhaps the SP shall set up a joint Labor Committee for the fight against fascism. This "Labor Committee" they did not envisage as a trade union body. It was at this meeting that Draper, their representative, stated, "We expect nothing from the labor movement at this time. The Socialists will have to act alone." Of course we rejected this, explaining that our orientation was towards forming a united front of unions and other large working-class organizations.

B. A united front mass meeting of both parties. We explained that this was unrealistic since it simply meant a proposal that we provide them with a platform and we preferred to speak from our own platform in party meetings and could see no benefit from a joint mass meeting.

C. A united membership meeting to discuss the antifascist struggle. Again we explained that they had been provided with ample opportunity to remain in the party and have full rights in discussion as an opposition faction. Since they treacherously split with the SWP, it was unreasonable for them to demand the rights of members within our organization.

D. United front picket lines against any future meeting Smith may hold. We gave them the same answer; that we were orienting to the formation of such a united front with the working-class organizations that really represented the mass of workers in the city and thereby the power of the workers in the city. As regards future demonstrations of Smith, we would appraise the question of purely party demonstrations on the basis of the relationship of forces at a given time.

E. They proposed blocs to pass resolutions in the unions. Here we agreed to consider such blocs on the basis of any concrete situation that offered possibilities along this line. They could cite only one, Local 9, Shipyard Workers. We could think of no other. In this union we had formed a bloc with a Negro militant, the vice-president of the state CIO, a former Stalinist, who had agreed to present our resolution. Nevertheless, we agreed to refer the question to our fraction with a recommendation that our fraction consult with their fraction; mainly because we were concerned with restraining them from any blundering interference with the arrangements we had made. This is precisely what occurred. Our fraction representative met with theirs. They arrogantly insisted on proposing their own resolution with their own speaker. We finally persuaded them to refrain from doing so until a far more effective arrangement could be put through. This was the extent of our bloc with the Shachtmanites in Local 9.

The united front is formed

Smith announced plans for his final rally for July 20th at the Shrine Auditorium at a small secret meeting in Clifton's Cafeteria. We had observers present at this meeting and were the first to spread the alarm throughout the labor movement and Jewish organizations. We called up representative individuals and appraised them of the plans of Smith. Immediately the movement for antifascist action was spurred forward. As we reported before, one Jewish newspaper called for a mass picket demonstration. A Jewish workers cultural organization pledged its 300 members in support of a picket line at the Shrine meeting. The pressure of our campaign was developing considerably in the CIO. The Stalinist rank and file and periphery were dissatisfied with the official policy.

The first news we heard of the development of a united front and a counterdemonstration for July 20th, came from Slim Connally, a Stalinist CIO leader, who told one of our comrades that the CIO was calling a counterdemonstration at the Olympic Auditorium on the same night as Smith's Shrine meeting. He told our comrade, a Negro trade unionist, to spread the word among the Negro people. Our comrade immediately came down to the Central Branch meeting of the party and announced the news.

At the same time we heard that a meeting of all antifascist organizations was to take place at the Royal Palms Hotel on Tuesday, July 17, to lay the plans for the final buildup for the Olympic Auditorium demonstration.

The Tuesday meeting proved to be an extremely representative gathering of the trade unions, racial minority organizations, religious and Hollywood groups. A sprinkling of bourgeois politicians decorated the occasion with the typical Stalinist attempt to distort a united front into a peoples' front masquerade. Official representatives of the CIO, AFL, and Railroad Brotherhoods were present. A good number of local unions, mostly CIO, were also represented. A mystery of sorts surrounds the question of precisely which organization took the initiative in calling this united front. Attorney-General Kenney and Assemblyman Albert Decker were assigned the roles of official chairman and convener. Our first information led us to believe that the CIO had called for the Olympic meeting and the Royal Palms united front gathering. This accounts for the fact that the *Militant* characterized the Olympic meeting as a CIO demonstration rather than a united front demonstration, at which the CIO, AFL, and Railroad Brotherhoods participated, together with racial organizations and other "community" groups. It is possible that the Stalinists started with the CIO as sponsor and then obscured its role when they found such widespread support from other organizations and individuals. In our opinion, organization control of the Olympic Auditorium meeting and the initiative in calling the Royal Palms meeting lies with the Stalinists. The question of which organization was officially responsible recedes into the background once it is clear that the Stalinists were the most powerful force which controlled the apparatus of both meetings. What then is our analysis of this set-up? Is it a genuine united front?

There can be no question that it was a real united front, but as is always the case with institutions that arise out of the reality of the struggle, as distinguished from textbook definitions, this concrete united front has its peculiarities, determined by the entire situation. The ground swell of workers' antifascist sentiment for action was sufficient to jar the official apparatus of labor and of the Stalinist party into action. This workers' sentiment, when combined with the state of excitement and anxiety of the Jewish organizations, proved sufficient to bring together in one Council an extremely wide representation of the labor movement and the racial minority groups. However, the movement of the workers from below has not yet reached the point where it could express itself in a united front of action which would be representative of the labor organizations from top to *bottom*. What was striking at the Tuesday Royal Palms meeting was the inordinate importance and weight held by political shysters, Hollywood stars, accidental figures, and the summits of the labor movement. There were too many religious quacks and too few factory workers. This signifies an early stage in the united front struggle against fascism. The

Stalinists are working might and main in this early stage to derail the movement; to switch it on to the path of peoples' frontism, to stifle the initiative of working-class ranks. This is the characteristic element of their policy at the Royal Palms and Olympic meetings.

The party in action

How did the party participate in this movement? We immediately declared our full support to the idea of a counterdemonstration against the fascists. Our leaflet calling for the workers to pack the Olympic Auditorium was the first announcement of the demonstration on the streets. The campaign that was organized during that one week in some respects surpassed the election campaign. The SEC declared a state of full mobilization, and that proved to be no idle phrase. It was understood by the overwhelming majority of the party membership to mean an extraordinary demand on their time and energy, and they acted accordingly.

The week was notable for our utilization of a long unused medium of agitation, the open air meeting, which has now become a regular feature of our campaign. We decided to launch a new series of radio broadcasts, and attempted to arrange the schedule in time to announce it to the workers gathered at the Olympic Auditorium; but we were blocked in this by the refusal of the broadcasting companies to sell us the time.

The first part of the week was concentrated on getting out the leaflet, beginning its mass distributions, preparing a mailing to 4,000 subscribers and contacts and in preparation for the Tuesday meeting. All our fractions were instructed to work wherever possible to represent their unions at the Tuesday meeting. In most cases the shortness of time prevented the democratic election of delegates and thereby cut down our own representation. Union officials would, as a rule, appoint one of their group to attend. Yet we had four trade union delegates at the united front meeting. We had three delegates from the party, and about thirty comrades participated as individual observers.

There were approximately 400 present at the Tuesday meeting. The night before at the SEC we had elaborated a three-point policy to be following by the party caucus. (1) Continue the united front after the Friday meeting as an organ of struggle against fascism; (2) For a preponderance of representatives of the labor movement on the speaker's rostrum. Instead of Hollywood celebrities, let's have the leaders of the labor movement, Green, Murray, and Lewis, fly out here and speak at the meeting; (3) We proposed the Olympic Auditorium demonstration should have a brief program and should then be transformed into a giant parade to march on the Shrine. The Olympic Auditorium is one mile from the Shrine. Our proposal was to march the parade past the Shrine in a peaceful display of antifascist strength and to demobilize a few blocks past the Shrine.

On Tuesday we had two speakers get the floor at the United Front meeting. Following a speaker from an Italian organization, who stated that if workers had organized in time and fought back, fascism would never have triumphed in Italy and Germany, Comrade Cappy got the floor and presented the proposal for adjourning the Olympic meeting early and parading to the Shrine. Then Comrade Tanner was recognized. She spoke for fifteen minutes, outlining the proposals of the party. The party proposal for a march became the pivotal point for all further discussion. Her speech was received with considerable applause as well as some subdued heckling from the Stalinists. The *People's World* reported the next day that "speaker after speaker" came out against Myra Weiss, leader of the local Trotskyites who had proposed a parade past the Shrine after a brief meeting at the Olympic.

In the course of a debate at the Wednesday party membership meeting Comrade Cappy developed the idea that our proposal for a march was adventuristic and represented a succumbing to the pressure of the Shachtmanites. The reporter for the SEC, Comrade Weiss, held that it was precisely this proposal which had marked off the left-wing of the United Front; that the proposal was entirely realistic; that it was feasible to call for the organization of an antifascist parade when the forces we were addressing this proposal to represented all the official organizations of the labor movement; that taking into account the real strength of the fascists, such a parade would have the effect of a powerful sledgehammer attack. It would weaken Smith immensely.

As for the comparison with the Shachtmanites, it was held that our difference with them was over the question of proceeding with a tiny force in an ineffective display of weakness against the fascists; whereas we were appealing to the strong workers' organizations to act against the fascists. Although it was not disputed that many tens of thousands of workers were still unaware of the character of the Smith movement, there were other tens of thousands, still in the minority, who were ready to take militant action once they saw a realistic possibility of doing so. An official decision of the labor movement to act, parade past the Shrine, would call forth a tremendous burst of enthusiasm and action from tens of thousands of militant workers in this area. Furthermore to underscore that we were not proposing a march led by us alone, we had stressed in our formulation of the proposal that if the majority of the united front opposed such a parade, we would be bound by that decision.

The Friday meeting

The attendance at the Olympic Auditorium meeting revealed the depth of the movement that had been aroused against Smith's activities. The antifascist workers, the Jewish, Negro, and other racial minority groups, were obviously looking to the Olympic meeting as a great force in the struggle to crush the fascists. The Auditorium was packed to the rafters with a huge overflow crowd of 5,000 on the outside. Seventeen-thousand would be a very safe estimate of the total attendance.

Across the platform of the meeting was paraded the usual Stalinist handpicked assortment of phony politicians, religious leaders, Hollywood stars, etc. However, the heads of the AFL and CIO Los Angeles Council spoke. The greatest ovation was received by Philip Connally, the head of the CIO Council. The most spirited applause occurred when the speakers struck a militant note. When Connally said: "We do not believe in free speech for the fascists," the enthusiasm of the audience reached its height.

What was most characteristic of the whole program and the meeting—and it went to about 11:30—was the fact that not one speaker told the workers what they should do in the struggle against Smith. Attorney General Kenney painted the picture of the war boom industries threatening to collapse, the danger of unemployment, the sharpening of a social crisis as a result of it; and cited this as the reason for Smith's activity in this area. He said: "The way to fight Smith and other fascists is to keep industry going at capacity with full employment." All he failed to do was to tell the audience how.

The Stalinists pushed to the fore the question of Rankin's forthcoming investigation of Hollywood. It became apparent that they are utilizing this united front, both at the Olympic meeting and at future meetings, to shield themselves from the red scare attack that the reactionaries are trying to whip up in Hollywood.

The Olympic meeting was the product of a real movement from below. The Stalinists are not capable of calling such meetings at will. When Philip Murray came to Los Angeles in 1943, the Stalinists, who were then trying to impress Murray, tried to gather a large meeting together at the Olympic with Hollywood stars featured and an enormous publicity campaign. However, the meeting was poorly attended with a very low level of enthusiasm.

It is hard to say what the composition of the Friday meeting was. The Stalinists and their periphery were there in full force. There was a strong middle-class professional grouping. Without doubt there were many thousands of industrial workers present and quite a large number of Negroes. Some comrades believe that the largest percentage of workers were turned away in the overflow crowd; those who couldn't arrive early enough due to working hours.

We distributed our leaflet in over 8,000 copies. The four proposals are the pivotal points around which we propose to agitate in the shops and the unions during the coming period. The slogans for antifascist shop committees we regard as extremely potent in possibilities. There, the initiative will more and more fall into our hands. In the last analysis, the united front that has emerged represents all the weaknesses of the existing state of the labor movement; the union tops disconnected from the workers in the shops, the Stalinist political and trade union apparatus, the heavy middle-class element. As the struggle sharpens, the party will bring the slogans of the left-wing of the united front into every factory where we have contact. At a certain point the formation of antifascist factory committees will provide the medium for the organization of vital combat forces. One of the possibilities of the formation of workers' defense guards is linked up with the factory committees, although it is not excluded that the workers' defense guards will have an initially neighborhood, or even racial minority origin.

The third point of our proposal is obviously the most immediate. It is our opinion that if we follow the right tactic with sufficient energy, we can meet the next wave of fascist activity with *labor demonstrations and mass picketing*. It is not a question of can we "get by" with some small picket lines of the "radical" parties. It is a question of how to mobilize masses of workers for struggle, without ignoring the reality of their existing organizations and leadership. Every party venture, every party tactic must be calculated to further this end.

The fourth point (the labor party) has become particularly timely after the results of the British elections and is now prominently lifted to the place of an independent and immediate campaign of agitation for the party as a whole.

All the comrades at the meeting reported that our leaflet was read carefully by those they could observe around them. Not one leaflet was found thrown away; this despite the fact that tremendous amounts of literature were being distributed at the entrances. Before the meeting our distributors succeeded in contacting a few new Shachtmanite recruits, who have since been followed up and look to be very promising.

The distribution squad was caught outside with the thousands of workers who couldn't get in, and engaged in many fruitful discussions in the street. After the police dispersed the crowds, we filled the available cars with contacts and brought them to the headquarters. When the others returned after the meeting, it was as if we had a mass meeting in our own hall. Although it was after midnight, the new workers contacted were anxious to hear a word from the party speakers.

Our observer at the Shrine meeting reported how Smith ascribed the poor attendance at his rally (5,000) to "the Communists and the Jews who had packed the streetcars en route to the Shrine and Olympic Auditoriums." Comrades Tanner and Weiss announced our determination to continue the open air meetings on the East Side and our plans to develop a free speech fight if the police interfered again as they had done earlier. Since then we have held three successful street meetings on the same corner without any further difficulties.

Summary and perspectives

The campaign is in a moment of lull. Smith has left town for speaking engagements in the East, promising to return soon. His threat to make Los Angeles a national headquarters was not carried out. It is not even a West Coast headquarters. For the moment he is working under the surface once again. How long will this last? Will he start a new campaign of meetings? Will someone else of the same caliber raise a new threat? These questions cannot be answered in detail.

We base ourselves on the inevitable development of further fascist activities. The reported rifle clubs in the valleys can become the point of departure for a new offensive in the antifascist campaign. We are investigating the activities of local supporters of Smith. Generally speaking, there is no lack of vigilante and fascist activities in Southern California. The party then prepares for a new big push in its campaign. What better preparation can there be than the assimilation of the lessons of the first stage of the campaign?

The contrast between our policy and the Shachtmanites had a clear and finished character. The two lines of policy were submitted to the test in a short time. It is useful and instructive to draw up a balance sheet.

The Shachtmanites proceeded by a superficial analogy to the Madison Square Garden demonstration of 1938. They "expected nothing from the labor movement at this time," and they thought that a mere signal from anyone was sufficient to bring a mass of anti-fascist workers into the streets. If one is serious about summoning masses to action, it must be conceded that they miscalculated on both counts.

The antifascist masses would not in these circumstances move against the Smith type of fascist movement without first exhausting the possibility of utilizing the defensive covering and power of their own mass organizations. In this they display a far better grasp of the difference between the Smith fascists and the German-American Bund than the Shachtmanites do. The militant workers did not answer the call to picket because they felt the need to move with and through the unions. Moreover they estimated that it was possible to get action from their organizations and proceeded to apply pressure. That is why we found that we were not alone in our efforts to push for the united front and for antifascist action in the unions. Everywhere other militants were following the same line.

Our tactic was fully confirmed by the course of events. The objective implications of Smith's activity were so ominous in the setting of the present economic and political situation, that the trade union officials, the Stalinists, the Negro and Jewish leaders could not fail to be alarmed. Our task was to hammer home the meaning of the fascist threat and to organize the pressure of the workers to force the organizations of labor onto the road of struggle.

It is necessary to understand clearly that the Shachtmanites did not simply add to the tactics we carried out, by organizing a picket line. They followed a totally different course. They could not see the reality or effectiveness of a struggle for the united front in the unions, and they had no conception whatsoever of a united front tactic with the Stalinists.

They complain: "You claimed you had no time for preparing a joint demonstration with us, but you were ready in the available time to act jointly with the Stalinists." Of course! In uniting with the WP we could calculate mainly on our own forces to act. For this we lacked time *and* the necessary relationship of forces. If we could unite with the Stalinists instead of the WP this would signify an enormous change in the relationship of forces and the time factor would alter accordingly. The Shachtmanites cannot understand that this is the reason why we fight for the united front with the Stalinists. It is not because we hate the WP worse than we hate the Stalinists, or because of our natural bureaucratic affinity for the Stalinists. It is because in one direction a mass of workers are concentrated; in the other, little more than a handful of renegades from Marxism.

This is not the place for an estimate of the antifascist campaigns of 1938–39. Certainly the demonstrations in New York and Los Angeles were of great significance. However, in my opinion the model of antifascist activity for the party is to be found in Minneapolis. The relative weight of their antifascist tactics as against the other ventures of the party is much greater precisely because they operated through the mass movement of the workers. It is this aspect of the Minneapolis experience that should be assimilated by the party now.

The question remains: Could anything have been lost by joining in a picket demonstration with the Shachtmanites at the Philharmonic on June 25th? Yes! A great deal would have been lost. Adding a few hundred to such a picket line would not have raised its effectiveness qualitatively. What was needed was a demonstration of the overwhelming preponderance labor possessed in the contest. Even the Olympic Auditorium demonstration accomplished this. By mobilizing 17,000 in a counter-demonstration to the fascist 5,000, a demoralizing blow was struck at them.

But could anything have been lost? In following such a tactic we would have become divorced from the mainstream of militant workers who were pressing hard on the lever to lift their organizations into action. By concentrating on helping them press this lever, we solidified our connection with them. Many workers were irritated and contemptuous of the policy of a "show of weakness." Had we followed that course we would be arguing to this day with the Stalinist workers about the question of whether the Trotskyists are "hotheads" and "ineffective." "Look how small their demonstration was. Why do they jump the gun?" As it is, we decisively reject responsibility for the WP antics. We point to our record of struggle for the united front and we propose action to the workers' organizations.

The perspective of the antifascist campaign is very broad and converges with other campaigns. This distinguishes it from the more narrow party campaigns with their succinct objectives and delimited time. We compensate for this by introducing into the broad campaign the element of organization objective whenever possible. When there is a lull we exploit it for analysis and preparation, rather than for artificial campaign-mongering. Right now campaign activity is confined to open air meetings. At the same time we are searching for an opening that will allow us to lift the struggle to a higher level. There is a possibility for organizing a meeting with a number of Jewish groups who hold militant positions on the tasks of the united front. In a bloc with them we could present our proposals for militant action at the next united front conference, which will occur on August 26th. If we mobilize the forces of the party and its sympathizers in the trade unions we can have a large group at the united front meeting. The same tactic can be developed toward Negro and Mexican organizations, who are keenly aware of the threat of fascism with its physical violence and terror. In the solidification of such a bloc lies the possibility of, in the next immediate period, calling united front demonstrations and picket lines.

In the next stage of the campaign, through the radio, through demonstrations, through the deepening of our united front tactics, we shall draw even closer to our banner the sympathetic periphery of *Militant* readers and contacts. We will recruit many of them. The party will grow stronger.

We want the comrades nationally to know that when the Los Angeles Local raised the slogan of "No headquarters for Smith in Los Angeles," we did so in deadly earnest. We are committed to this slogan to the marrow of our bones. For the Socialist Workers Party the struggle against fascism is to the death.

AUGUST 7, 1945

2. Minneapolis picket line smashes fascist rally
By Barbara Bruce

Minneapolis, Minnesota, Aug. 22—A united labor movement stopped fascist Gerald L.K. Smith from speaking last night in Minneapolis. More than 1,500 pickets from AFL, CIO, and railroad unions, along with members of veterans, Jewish, Negro and working class political organizations, including the Socialist Workers Party, rallied in a fighting mass demonstration against America's No. 1 fascist leader.

When Smith's goons assaulted several pickets outside the fascists' meeting place at the Leamington Hotel, the aroused workers stormed the meeting hall and routed Smith and his followers in a pitched battle.

Smith's talk was originally booked for the Hennepin County Republican Club rooms at 703 Third Avenue South. Long before meeting time, an organized picket line was formed under the direction of Walter Frank, secretary of AFL Lathers Union No. 190, and representative of the Minneapolis Central Labor Union, who acted as picket captain.

Assistant picket captains were Henry A. Schultz, representing the Brotherhood of Railroad Trainmen, Lodge 102, and Earl Cluka, financial secretary of United Electrical, Radio, and Machine Workers, representing the Hennepin County CIO Council.

Reprinted from the August 31, 1946, issue of the *Militant*.

'Stop fascism!'
Scores of banners carried by the pickets had been distributed by the united labor committee. They carried such slogans as "Race Hatred Is Fascism"; "Stop Fascism and G.L.K. Smith"; "Don't Be a Sucker for Fascists"; "Don't Support Hitler's Agent—Keep Away." By agreement of the committee in charge, each organization carried only one placard.

Among the organizations carrying their own banners were the National Association for the Advancement of Colored People; the Workers Defense League; the Minneapolis AFL Central Labor Union; the Minneapolis AFL Building Trades Council; the American Veterans Committee; the American Youth for Democracy; the Socialist Workers Party; the Communist Party; and the Minneapolis Jewish Action Committee.

Prominent in the picket line was the banner of the Socialist Workers Party proclaiming, "American Workers Do Not Want a Hitler—STOP Gerald L.K. Smith."

March through loop
A group of Smith's followers had gathered at the Third Avenue address, waiting for the door to be unlocked. Smith's secretary, Renata Legant, moved among the known Smith supporters in the crowd

and told them to assemble in the ballroom of the Leamington Hotel.

When the [antifascist] picket captains gave the signal, the huge body of pickets marched down the street to the hotel three blocks away singing "Solidarity Forever" and shouting "Down With the Fascists!" As the picket line moved toward the hotel, some of the Smith goons attempted to break up the line. Several of the pickets were attacked and knocked to the sidewalk. When the attackers fled into the hotel, the pickets stormed in after them.

Surging through the lobby, the pickets were met by a knot of fascists who attempted to bar the way to the ballroom where the meeting was to be held. With a mighty push, the Smith supporters were brushed aside and the pickets plunged on like a great tidal wave toward the meeting hall.

Charging through a barricade of chairs which the fascists had thrown up to prevent the pickets from entering the hall, the shouting mass of labor antifascists made their way into the ballroom. In their frantic retreat, the fascists left broken chairs, tables, lamps, and mirrors in their wake. Dozens of Smith's supporters fled through the windows. Those remaining in the hall scuttled to one corner of the room and huddled there.

Workers take over

At the call of the picket captain, Walter Frank, all the pickets were seated. Frank's announcement that no Smith meeting would be held was greeted with resounding cheers. He reported that the hotel manager had refused to let Smith's meeting take place and ordered the fascists out, since the ballroom had been obtained under false pretenses. One of Smith's followers had rented the hall in the name of the "Northwest Pioneers."

The assembled pickets were then instructed to march in a body to the Minneapolis Courthouse where an antifascist rally would be held. A rearguard of pickets was left at the hotel to see that instructions of the manager were carried out.

Smith came out of hiding only after the pickets left. He attempted to hold a meeting in the hotel lobby but only a handful of people remained. In one of his usual attacks on the labor movement and minorities, Smith declared to his followers that the demonstration was the work of "Jewish terrorists and Communists."

Victory meeting

Following their captains' orders, the pickets marched to the courthouse, still singing, and chanting "Down with Smith!" Hundreds of workers, white and Negro, Jewish and gentile, Protestant and Catholic, along with veterans and students, poured into the hall. Here they cheered the picket captains who praised the conduct of the pickets throughout the demonstration and their magnificent defense against the fascist attackers.

When Frank concluded a stirring address by stating that "the CIO, AFL, railroad brotherhoods, and independent unions must join forces in a common struggle against reaction in America," the hall rang with applause.

Others who spoke were: Milton Siegel, field representative and Vice President, District 2, of the CIO United Packinghouse Workers; Henry A. Schultz, spokesman for Lodge 102, Railroad Trainmen; Henry Piper, associate editor of *Labor Review*, official organ of the Minneapolis Central Labor Union; and Jerrold Stoll, American Veterans' Committee representative. The meeting closed with a pledge to continue the organized fight against fascism in America. The crowd left singing "Solidarity."

Great tradition lives

This inspiring antifascist labor battle shows that the great tradition of working-class solidarity and militancy, built in Minneapolis during the thirties by the famous Minneapolis Drivers Local 544, is still alive. The spirit of labor struggle that the Roosevelt administration and AFL Teamsters President Tobin tried to crush during the war by the imprisonment of the Trotskyist leaders of Local 544 has survived.

Those leaders, like Vincent R. Dunne, played a prominent role in last night's antifascist fight.

In the 1941 Minneapolis Labor Trial, the basis of one charge against him and the other 17 defendants was their advocacy of union defense guards to defend labor meetings from fascist attacks.

3. Comments on the Minneapolis antifascist campaign
By Vincent R. Dunne

The following is an excerpt from the transcript of remarks made by Vincent Dunne to a class on fascism held in Minneapolis on December 30, 1963. Dunne was a founding member of the Communist League of America, the first American Trotskyist organization. He was a central leader of the Minneapolis strikes of 1934. At the time of the 1946 antifascist campaign, he was national labor secretary of the SWP. He was an active leader of the SWP from its founding in 1938 to his death in 1970.

The fascists tried to come back here, long after we were no longer the heroes of the labor movement, after we were imprisoned for our opposition to the war. They came back and tried to rent the auditorium in Gerald L.K. Smith's name to put on an anticommunist demonstration.

The leader of the Minneapolis labor movement, the Central Labor Union, had become pretty quiet by that time. They were lined up with the Democratic Party, turned over everything to labor boards, were quite satisfied, and didn't want any more trouble. The former leaders of the truckers were no longer the leaders of the labor movement, but we had been delegates to the Central Labor Union and we knew the leaders well enough to impress them with the danger of this fascist meeting.

We were for the city turning over the auditorium to Gerald L.K. Smith and for organizing a demonstration against him. But they denied him the auditorium. He finally got quite a big hall on Third Avenue.

Now the Minnesota Jewish Council, a petty-bourgeois group, urged the trade union leadership to ignore Smith. Many of the leaders in the Central Labor Union went along with this.

A meeting had been called for the Jewish leaders and the trade union movement. We sent a committee over there of former leaders in the drivers union and asked them to reconsider this. They had agreed not to demonstrate. Give Smith the silent treatment, they said. We said, the silent treatment is no good in a case like this. You've got to go down and picket that place. We had the support of two or three of the leaders of the Central Labor Union on this.

A second meeting was scheduled. We turned around the whole meeting that had been called to give the fascists the silent treatment. In the end, one of the rail unions called a demonstration that became a demonstration of the entire trade union movement.

Even the Communist party participated that time, the only united front I remember with the Communist party here. They were quite numerous in Minneapolis. They had some union posts. They supported this. It was overwhelmingly accepted by the rank and file of the trade union movement, so they couldn't back down.

The trade union movement had charge of the picket line. Many of our comrades were picket captains. Thousands of people demonstrated in front of Smith's meeting hall. Finally, Smith gave up the idea of having a meeting there and sent in word that they were going to the main ballroom of the Leamington Hotel.

We were aware of this and we sent our pickets down to challenge them when they came out the back door. Pickets were strung along Third Avenue and several other streets so that whatever way they went, we'd catch them.

At the Leamington Hotel, they began to attack us. They sent squads out to brutally attack our pickets. We fought back and when the main body of our picket line got there, there was a melee in front of the hotel. We just marched right into the hotel, challenged them right at their door, drove their sluggers back into the ballroom. Some of the people at the front of the line—I wasn't there at the moment—broke in the big old doors of the ballroom. Chandeliers went down, everything went down, as the fascists went out the back door. They've never been back here since.

There are lessons to be drawn from this. That is the way the fascist threat must be met. And that can only be done by a mass movement of the workers. It can't be done by petty-bourgeois individuals giving fascists the "silent treatment."

III. PROTESTS AGAINST THE AMERICAN NAZI PARTY

With the decline of McCarthyism, fascist and incipient fascist groups were consigned for the time being to the lunatic fringe of American politics, although they occasionally made headlines by participating in struggles against school integration in the South.

One of the most exotic fascist groups formed in this period was the American Nazi Party, formed in 1956 by George Lincoln Rockwell, an ex-army officer. Openly identifying with Hitler and the German fascist movement, Rockwell was cut off from support from even the most reactionary sectors of the American masses. Rockwell attempted to gain some publicity by several public appearances in 1960 and 1961. The result was a series of protests which the SWP supported and helped to build.

The experience of McCarthyism and the widespread revulsion against the antidemocratic policies of Stalinism led the SWP to place greater stress on its opposition to official restrictions on the legal rights of Nazis. Such restrictions could only add to the government's armory of repressive weapons against antifascist and working class dissenters. United-front, mass-action tactics continued to be the keynote in organizing antifascist action.

The following materials deal with two incidents. The letter from James P. Cannon and the two items from the *Militant* which follow deal with Rockwell's attempt to schedule a rally in New York City's Union Square on July 4, 1960, and court actions arising from it.

The letter from Joseph Hansen to Larry Trainor deals with an antifascist demonstration in Boston on December 16, 1960. Trainor was a leader and activist in the SWP for forty years until his death in 1975.

Rockwell was murdered in 1967 by the leader of a splitoff from his Nazi group.

1. Letter from James P. Cannon to Tom Kerry, June 23, 1960

Dear Tom,

I learned by way of radio and TV last night that Mayor Wagner denied the preposterous American "Nazi" outfit a permit to hold a meeting in Union Square; and that he said the people "would stone them out of town." Then the TV report showed the scene of the attempt to mob the American Nazi leader outside the courtroom. I am disturbed by this little off-beat episode and wondering rather anxiously to what extent, if any, we were mixed up in it and how the paper is going to handle the occurrences in its report.

No doubt it was "a famous victory." But a victory for what and for whom? Certainly not a victory for the right of free speech and assembly as guaranteed by the Bill of Rights to which we are firmly, and I hope sincerely, devoted. For us, I take it, under any reasonably normal conditions, free speech is a principle—not only before the revolution but also after it, when the workers' government becomes stabilized. But free speech is also a practical necessity for us, of particular burning importance when we are fighting as a small minority for the right to be heard.

We certainly didn't win anything to sustain this right by Mayor Wagner's decision. It sets a dangerous precedent. The reasons he gave for denying the constitutional rights of the American "Nazi" screwballs, and his incitement to violence against them, can be applied just as well and just as logically to us or any other minority. We will be greatly handicapped in fighting against such discriminations if we give direct or even indirect sanction to this treatment of others. People who demand free speech and constitutional rights for themselves but want to deny it for others do not get much public sympathy when their own rights are denied.

This was demonstrated quite convincingly by the public and labor indifference to the persecution of the Stalinists in the period since the cold war began. The Stalinist record of claiming rights for themselves and denying them, or trying to deny them, to their opponents boomeranged against them. It gave other people a reason, or an excuse, to stand aside or even to join the hue and cry against the persecuted Stalinists on the ground that "free speech is all right, but not for communists."

I don't think the "Nazi" crackpots lost anything by this New York decision. They got a lot of nationwide free advertising, and a chance to appear as a persecuted minority, and the ground to appeal for funds and recruits. If they had a cause with any semblance of appeal to popular sympathy they would profit by this flagrant denial of their rights under the Bill of Rights.

The whole episode is quite obviously a tempest in a teapot. It has very little relation to social and political realities in present day America. But there is a *symptomatic* significance and we should ponder it. The problem, in one form or another, will come up again and again; and we must not stumble into an improvised policy each time. We have to have a *line*. As I see it, our line is free speech. We have to fight for it and convince other people that we mean it. With truth on our side, we have the most to gain by freedom of discussion and the most to lose by its suppression. It is true that, as the class struggle develops, we will have to fight the fascists, and not only with words. But this will not be a fight to deprive the fascists of the right to speak and to meet, but a defensive fight to prevent them from interfering with the rights of the workers.

Fraternally,
s/James P. Cannon

2. Wagner hands Rockwell an issue

George Lincoln Rockwell, the American Nazi who advocates Hitler's gas-chamber way of ending "the menace" of "Jews and Negroes," announced June 27 that he is calling off his plans to stage a rally in New York's Union Square on July 4. At the same time he is pressing the New York Civil Liberties Union to protect his right to speak.

"The New York Civil Liberties Union hates my guts," he is quoted as saying, "but they have a terrific stake in protecting my right to speak. They can't afford to protect the rights of Communists and Jews, and look the other way while my rights are being denied."

Mayor Wagner is to be blamed for handing this grievance to Hitler's American admirer. At a court hearing June 22 over an injunction to bar city officials from issuing a permit for Rockwell's rally, a crowd expressed its opposition to Rockwell's provocative statements in such vigorous fashion that the police intervened and rushed the Nazi out of town. Utilizing this incident as a pretext, Wagner denied the permit for the rally.

The groups that first took notice of Rockwell's plan to stage a Nazi rally in Union Square did not question his right to free speech. The Committee to Protest Racist Defamation, for instance, did not seek to stop Rockwell from speaking. The New York Local of the Socialist Workers Party likewise did not question his right to address a crowd in Union Square. What the antifascist forces proposed was that everyone interested in the issue should come down to Union Square on July 4 and exercise their right of free speech, too, by expressing their opinions of Rockwell's racist views.

Editorial reprinted from the July 4, 1960, issue of the *Militant*.

Conrad J. Lynn, representing the Committee to Protest Racial Defamation, put it like this in a letter to the Department of Parks in which he pressed for a permit for a public meeting in Union Square on July 4 to answer the Nazis: "We believe that evil thought must be allowed to express itself as long as truth is free to combat it."

The *New York Post*, after first publicizing the Nazi rally, closed its columns to further news until the court incident occurred. Then, in an editorial, it advocated a policy of silence toward Nazis like Rockwell. The logic of this view is that opponents of would-be American Hitlers should not exercise their own right of free speech in the form of rallies—or even discussion in the press!

The latest moves are to illegalize the American Nazis and put them on the so-called "subversive" list. New York State Supreme Court Justice Louis L. Friedman signed a temporary injunction June 28 "restraining" the party and its commander "from engaging in any subversive activities in New York State," according to the press. The judge also accepted a disorderly conduct complaint made by the Jewish War Veterans and signed a warrant of arrest for Rockwell if and when he comes back to the state.

In our opinion, such moves are wrong on two counts. First of all, they are infringements of the right of free speech and the right to engage in politics. Such infringements of anyone's rights, no matter who it may be, inevitably put in question everyone's democratic rights. Didn't America learn that to its cost in the witch-hunting days of President Truman and Senator McCarthy?

Secondly, such moves are ineffective in counteracting the poisonous racist views of the Rockwells. In fact, by victimizing them, it helps them win sympathy.

We think the most effective way of handling these vermin is to keep them out in the open, to meet them in the public forum and through the exercise of democratic rights, including free speech and free political activity, to defeat them before they can get started as a serious menace.

To follow any other course is to betray lack of confidence in democratic rights and democratic institutions.

3. No victory for Nazis
By Joseph Hansen

On February 14 the Appellate Division in a 4-to-1 decision handed down a verdict in New York that was interpreted by the capitalist press as a victory for George Lincoln Rockwell, head of the swastika-wearing "American Nazis" party. Actually the grounds of the decision favored Rockwell's opponents, the defenders of civil liberties and democratic rights in America.

Last summer Rockwell applied for a permit to hold a rally in New York's Union Square on July 4. It was denied by Commissioner Newbold Morris on the ground that a riot would result.

The American Civil Liberties Union took up the case and carried it to State Supreme Court Justice Henry Epstein. He upheld the commissioner.

Justice Charles D. Breitel voiced the majority opinion of the Appellate Division in upsetting Epstein's ruling. Breitel held that it was unconstitutional to deny any minority the right to voice its opinion.

"The unpopularity of views," said Justice Breitel, "their shocking quality, their obnoxiousness, and even their alarming impact are not enough. Otherwise the preacher of any strange doctrine could be stopped; the antiracist himself could be suppressed, if he undertakes to speak in 'restricted' areas; and one who asks that public schools be opened indiscriminately could be lawfully suppressed, if only he chose to speak where persuasion is needed most."

Reprinted from the March 6, 1961, issue of the *Militant*.

Fear of a "riot" was the Wagner administration's excuse for denying Rockwell his democratic rights. They pointed to the fact that many New York workers were preparing to appear at Union Square to protest Rockwell's views.

But the organization that initiated the protest movement did not deny Rockwell's democratic right to hold the obnoxious rally. On the contrary, they recognized the right.

This was the stand taken by the Committee to Protest Racist Defamation, headed by the well-known civil-rights attorney Conrad J. Lynn, which sought a permit from the city authorities to hold a protest meeting in Union Square on July 4 from 10 a.m. to 2 p.m., preceding the 3 p.m. Nazi rally. The *Militant* backed this position when it supported the appeal for a big turnout at the protest meeting.

The city's denial of a permit to Rockwell set a dangerous precedent which, unless it is upset by the courts, will most certainly be used at a future time against organizations holding views diametrically opposed to those of the Nazis.

When Rockwell learned of the ruling by the Appellate Division, he immediately wired Commissioner Morris a request to hold a rally in Union Square at 10 a.m. May 1. He told the press that he had 50 or 60 "troopers" in training at Arlington, Va. for the rally "and we should have them in top condition."

When asked what he intended to speak about, he answered, "The race issue and anti-Communism . . . the overwhelming Jewish participation in Communism." He added that he was scheduling the rally for 10 a.m. "so that all these little Jews who try to meet ahead of us will have to get up early."

It is doubtful that Rockwell will get a permit for a rally in Union Square by May 1, since the city is now appealing to the State Court of Appeals. However, the ACLU is prepared to take the case to the U.S. Supreme Court.

If the ACLU succeeds in finally winning and Rockwell ultimately gets a permit to appear in Union Square, there is no doubt many thousands of New Yorkers will be down real early to exercise their own democratic right to protest Rockwell's provocative efforts to convert Hitler into an example for America to follow.

4. Letter from Joseph Hansen to Larry Trainor, February 6, 1961

Boston
Dear Larry:

Yes, we received the article about the demonstration against the Nazis together with the clippings and copies of the leaflet that was distributed.

I thought the article was well written and gave a very dramatic and vivid picture of what happened.

However, we thought it politically inadvisable to print the article; and instead wrote a short account based on the total material sent us. Aside from its shortness the main difference between the printed article and the one submitted is the line. In the *Militant* we felt it absolutely necessary to indicate what the party position is in relation to Rockwell's outfit. For example, the article sent us did not indicate that we do not oppose the democratic right of the Nazis to demonstrate. The *Harvard Crimson*, however, did report that "most of the students said they felt that the Nazis had a right to picket the theater, but upheld their own picketing as 'the only way we can protest against what they stand for.'" We considered this very important evidence that this was the attitude taken by the Boston branch of the SWP. The fact that it was reported by the *Harvard Crimson* made it all the more impressive.

I should like to call your attention to some differences in the way the New York local handled the Nazi demonstrators and the way the Boston branch went about it.

In New York, the SWP at no time assumed leadership of the counterdemonstration or even sought leadership. No leaflets were put out in the name of the SWP. The reason for this was that in view of the relative size of the party it would be an illusion to think that we can directly take leadership of the struggle against fascism. Our role is to urge the mass organizations to engage in this struggle.

To attempt to bypass the mass organizations can only sow illusions in our own ranks about our real strength and our real role; and insofar as it is noted by the members of other organizations it can create the illusion that the SWP will handle the job; they don't need to worry about it.

We did help to create a committee that called for a counterdemonstration and this committee succeeded in getting some big organizations to take action.

Another point of difference concerns the estimate of the Rockwell outfit. Does this represent incipient American fascism? I do not think so. The real American fascists look more like Mayor Hague, Senator McCarthy, possibly Senator Goldwater. It can be put down with absolute assurance that in no case will they wear Nazi uniforms, swastikas, and praise Hitler. To picture Rockwell's outfit as representing American fascism thus helps create the illusion that the real fascists, when they show up, will be identifiable with similar ease and will similarly openly stir up the most violent antipathies (including those of the most patriotic Americans).

Finally, in everything the New York local did, it stressed the fact that Rockwell's democratic rights were not being challenged. On the contrary. The counterdemonstrators were similarly exercising their democratic rights.

Aside from the question of principle involved in this, it would be a great political mistake to permit our worst foes to maneuver us into the position of seeming to deny democratic rights to others, no matter who, and to claim them only for ourselves. The consequences of this mistake is that we put ourselves into position to become the very next victims.

We had a discussion about this in the PC last June and Jim wrote us his opinions. I suggest you check the PC minutes for July 20, 1960, which included two letters (dated June 14 and June 23) from Jim.

With best regards,
Joseph Hansen

IV. THE STRUGGLE AGAINST RACISM AND FASCISM TODAY

New racist groups developed in the 1970s in opposition to efforts to achieve school desegregation through busing. Academicians like Jensen and Shockley found new audiences for pseudoscientific "theories" about the genetic inferiority of Black people. The atmosphere created by such forces stirred fascist groups into new activity.

Some radicals argued that antiracist counteractions should try to prevent racists and fascists from speaking. They claimed that free speech does not apply to such views. Focusing primarily on the free speech aspect of the question, YSA leader Malik Miah proposed a different strategy in a speech given in May 1975.

Free speech and the fight against the ultraright
By Malik Miah

Malik Miah is the former national chairperson of the Young Socialist Alliance and a member of the National Committee of the Socialist Workers Party. This article is based on a report he made to the June 7–10, 1975, plenum of the YSA National Committee. It is reprinted from the August 1975 issue of the *International Socialist Review*, which appeared as a supplement to the August 1, 1975 issue of the *Militant*.

The past year has seen a sharpening of racist discrimination and violence nurtured by the government, from President Ford down to the local school boards and police departments.

The government and corporations are trying to force Black people and other oppressed minorities to bear the greatest burden of the current depression, through discriminatory layoffs and cutbacks in welfare funds, child care, and education.

As part of this racist offensive, the politicians, media, and police have cooperated to encourage racist violence aimed at beating back the civil rights gains won by Black people in the past. The spearhead of this campaign has been in Boston, where the school committee and the racist organization ROAR (Restore Our Alienated Rights) have tried to physically prevent the implementation of school desegregation.

The racist offensive by the government and employers has been the breeding ground for other racist fanatics and right-wing and fascist organizations.

In West Virginia a reactionary movement has arisen to try to eliminate scientific textbooks and books by Black authors from the public schools.

There has been increased activity—including violent activity—by the Ku Klux Klan, the American Nazis, and other rightist outfits. Both the Klan and the Nazis sent organizers to Boston last fall when the desegregation struggle broke out, sensing fertile ground for their program of hate and violence. In Los Angeles, Nazi and right-wing Cuban exile groups have waged a bombing campaign against socialist organizations, Palestinian groups, and civil liberties groups.

This rise of racist and right-wing activity has extended onto the campuses as well. The Black-inferiority theories of academics such as William Shockley and Arthur Jensen are widely propagated.

The Klan and the Nazis are both on stepped-up recruiting drives, sending speakers to campuses.

In response to the general racist offensive, the NAACP, the National Student Coalition Against Racism (NSCAR), the Young Socialist Alliance, the Socialist Workers party, and many other groups have joined together in organizing antiracist demonstrations and meetings around the country. Most effective so far was the May 17 antiracist march in Boston.

On the campuses, students have been faced with the question of how best to answer such racist or fascist elements when they come to try to spread their influence. Over the past year the Young Socialist Alliance has helped organize a number of effective actions against racist academics and rightwing hucksters on the campuses, for example, at Yale University and at St. Cloud State College in Minnesota.

In each case the YSA began from the point of view that the most effective way to deal with these racists was through a campaign of education and broadly sponsored protest actions. The aim is to win over the majority of students in a massive repudiation of the racists and rightists, to demoralize them, defeat their organizing drives, and drive them back into their ratholes. Part of this strategy is to win the support of Black community organizations and unions, which are the social forces that have the greatest power to stop racist and fascist violence.

Other organizations have taken a different approach, advocating the tactic of shouting down racist and right-wing speakers or attempting to physically break up their meetings. Some also call on the school administration to ban these speakers from campus because of their reactionary ideas.

Variations on this general position are held by the Maoist Revolutionary Student Brigade, the Progressive Labor party, and the Spartacus Youth League. The SYL, for example, puts forward the slogan, "No platform for the fascists," and denies what it calls the "supposed 'right to freedom of speech'" of fascist groups.

In fighting the racists off the campus as well, these groups oppose the strategy of building mass mobilizations against the reactionaries. In Boston, for example, the Progressive Labor party favors militaristic confrontations by small groups with South Boston racists, rather than supporting the strategy of mass action embodied in the NAACP May 17 demonstration. The RSB boycotted the May 17 action. The Spartacist League, which is allied with the SYL, attended the demonstration of 15,000, but attacked it as "impotent."

The increasingly dangerous role played by the racist and rightist organizations makes it important for all opponents of racism and supporters of democratic rights to consider carefully how best to combat them.

In deciding what tactics are most effective, it is useful to look first at what these racist and fascist gangs represent in a historical sense. This will reveal what the antiracist forces are up against in deciding to take these groups on. What tactics to employ today will then come more clearly into focus.

The situation in the United States today is, of course, not one of a large-scale rise of fascism. There are no mass fascist organizations. The existing ultrarightist organizations, such as the Nazis, can do little more than conduct propaganda—as vicious as it may be—and resort to isolated, small-scale acts of violence. They are conscious purveyors of fascist views, proclaiming Hitler as their hero. In this form they are unacceptable to the masses in the United States.

More important now is the racist violence of groups such as ROAR in Boston, with its friends in the school committee and city hall, as well as the step-up in racist police brutality.

It can be expected that such groups will grow as the economic, social, and political crisis deepens. The United States is entering a period of a qualitatively deeper economic crisis than it has ever faced before. This is reflected in the fact that the current recession is deeper than any since the Great Depression and in the fact that it is part of a world recession. Even when the country comes out of the current downturn, the probability is that there will be shorter and shorter intervals between even more drastic downturns.

It is this type of situation—prolonged economic uncertainties and crisis—that is a precondition for the rise of a full-fledged fascist movement.

Fascism is a specific social phenomenon exemplified most clearly by the movements and regimes headed by the German Nazis and Mussolini's Blackshirts. It is important to use the term scientifically and to distinguish between the rise of small groups with a fascist ideology on the one hand, and the rise of a mass fascist movement or the imminent threat of a fascist regime taking power on the other.

Those who loosely called the Nixon administration "fascist," for example, are not likely to be taken seriously when they try to sound the alarm about the real thing.

Some of the most important characteristics of the rise of a fascist movement are:

1) A fascist movement is a mass movement based primarily on sections of the population standing between the two most powerful classes—the working class and the class of big capitalists. These "in-between" layers include small businesspeople and shopkeepers, professional people, farmers, and higher-level government functionaries. Another layer that is always a prime recruiting ground for the fascists is the police and army officers.

Sections of the working class can also be attracted to a fascist movement, especially the most privileged layers, and the most degraded layers, who are demoralized by unemployment or driven by poverty and hopelessness to antisocial acts.

2) A fascist movement feeds on the despair and frenzy that grip these layers of the population as a result of severe economic crisis, as their shops are squeezed out of business, their standard of living is slashed, or their means of livelihood threatened.

Fascist leaders use "antiestablishment" demagogy—sometimes even "socialist" or "revolutionary"-sounding rhetoric—to appeal to the dissatisfaction of the masses of people with the status quo. Thus the German fascists called themselves National *Socialists*. Fascists try to turn the anger of all those threatened with ruin by the capitalist crisis against the oppressed racial minorities and organized labor.

In this country, the approach of fascist organizations in the 1930s and 1940s was to claim to be the representatives of the "little man" against both the big capitalists and the "communists," directing their fire especially at Blacks, Jews and "big labor."

In his book *Fascism and Big Business*, Daniel Guerin points out that "fascism's game is to call itself anticapitalist without seriously attacking capitalism."

3) Fascists appeal to all the backward, obscurantist traditions, customs, and prejudices that have been deeply embedded in people through the repressive nature of all class society. Racism, sexism, superstition, mysticism, and national chauvinism are key weapons used by the fascist demagogues.

4) When a fascist movement becomes powerful enough to move toward taking governmental power, it means that major sections of the ruling capitalist class have decided in favor of giving the fascists full rein. It means the big banks and corporations have begun large-scale financing of the fascist groups.

This occurs when the economic crisis brings forth massive resistance on the part of the working class, and the capitalists see fascism as the only possible means of maintaining their rule. In effect they resort to a form of civil war to beat the working class into submission. The troops on the side of capitalism in this civil war are supplied by the fascist-led mass movement.

Thus fascism is not simply a new form of dictatorial rule. New police-state methods are not sufficient to defeat a strong, organized workers movement. The ruling class needs on its side the added force of the desperate middle class and backward workers. Through mass terror, murder, and other forms of intimidation carried out by these forces, the capitalist class aims at completely crushing, atomizing, and demoralizing the labor movement.

In general the capitalists would prefer not to have to resort to fascism. It is much more efficient for them to rule "democratically" through mass illusions in their system. But as the workers movement grows and develops in face of social crisis, their fear of socialist revolution makes the step a necessity for them.

However, the ruling class does not make the move in one leap. It begins with a process of increased attacks on the democratic rights of the workers—through legal repressive measures as well as extralegal ones, including small-scale collaboration with rightist groups.

5) Leon Trotsky explained that the reason fascism triumphed in Italy in 1922 and in Germany in 1933 was because of a default in leadership of

the working class by the Communist and Socialist parties.

The Russian revolution of 1917 demonstrated that the middle classes do not have to be won by reaction. If the workers organizations are able to project a bold, revolutionary program, a way forward out of the crisis, they can win the middle layers over to the anticapitalist struggle, just as the Bolsheviks won over decisive sections of the Russian peasantry.

The defeat of fascism is only possible in the final analysis with the defeat of capitalism. The question of who should rule will be decided in major class battles. This means a revolutionary socialist combat party must be built to lead the workers to accomplish this task.

But if the workers' leadership is indecisive and incapable of uniting the class to exert its full power, then the middle layers can become embittered against the workers movement and turn elsewhere in search of radical solutions.

In Germany the Stalinized Communist party took the disastrous position that the Social Democratic party was just as bad as the fascists. The CP refused to organize a united-front struggle with the Social Democrats, and Hitler's regime of terror triumphed without a struggle from the workers.

Trotsky wrote in 1940: "In all the countries where fascism became victorious, we had before the growth of fascism and its victory, a wave of radicalism of the masses; of the workers and the poorer peasants and farmers, and of the petty bourgeois class. . . . Only after these . . . tremendous waves, did Fascism become a big movement. There are no exceptions to this rule—Fascism comes only when the working class shows complete incapacity to take into its own hands the fate of society."

The name or forms under which a fascist movement might arise in this country cannot be predicted. But it is likely that an American fascist movement will not simply ape the German or Italian fascists, as the American Nazis do. It won't identify with hated figures like Hitler. It will be camouflaged, its features emerging from the American class struggle and American prejudices.

An American fascist movement might look more like ROAR (although ROAR is not now fascist) than a group sporting helmets and swastikas. Or it might emerge from sections of the Democratic or Republican parties, like Joseph McCarthy or Mayor Frank Hague of Jersey City, New Jersey, who, Leon Trotsky thought, could be designated a fascist.

It could also be noted that a fascist movement might incorporate elements like the National Caucus of Labor Committees, a group that evolved from a socialist organization to a fascist-type group, just as Mussolini did. Under cover of radical-sounding rhetoric about a CIA-Rockefeller plot and gimmicky tax schemes, this group has carried out thug attacks on the Communist party, the SWP and YSA, and trade unionists. It issues vicious, racist hate sheets against Blacks and Puerto Ricans, and opposes all strikes. It has unusually generous financial sources that allow it to send organizers to other countries.

The racist and right-wing groups we see today are breeding grounds of what can become a capitalist-backed mass extralegal force aimed at attacking and eliminating the organizations and democratic rights of the labor movement, the Black movement, and all the oppressed.

This is the full dimension of the problem before the antiracist movement. Already we see that the current racist offensive, abetted by the racist and right-wing groups, is an attack on the most militant section of the working class, Black people.

It is clear from history that the threat represented by the racist and rightist groups cannot be defeated by small groups. The only effective counterstrategy is to unite the labor movement, the Black movement, and their allies in countermobilizations that make it politically and physically impossible for the racist and right-wing groups to get away with their violent attacks on the democratic rights of others.

In the face of racist mobilizations, the antiracist movement today should exercise its democratic right to counterdemonstrate in protest. In face of right-wing violence, the antiracist forces have the democratic right of self-defense—which should, however, be exercised judiciously through forms adapted to the specifics of the situation.

The way to beat back these forces is to outmobilize them in the streets, to show them that they are a minority and cannot intimidate the opponents of racism. This is the case because their goal is precisely to strike fear into those on the side of working people and Black people.

Even though there is no mass fascist movement today, the debate over how to combat existing racist and right-wing groups is of great importance. Experiences gained by the antiracist movement today will be preparation for larger confrontations to come, contributing to the development of a leadership of the working class and oppressed minorities competent to defeat the fascists in future battles in the struggle for socialist revolution.

The struggles taking place on the campuses can play an important role in building the general antiracist countermobilization. Campus struggles will be an aid to antiracist movements off the campus, such as for school desegregation. And, on the other hand, forces from the working class and the Black community can be drawn into aiding the students' actions.

With the full implications of the antiracist struggle in mind, the problems with the "no platform for fascists" position—the position that racist or fascist meetings should be banned or disrupted—become clear.

First of all, the danger presented by these reactionary organizations does not arise primarily from their speaking and expounding their ideas. It arises from their violent *actions* in violation of the democratic rights of others—such as the ROAR lynch-type mobs that have stoned and beaten children and other Black people in Boston, the Nazi bombings in Los Angeles, and the Ku Klux Klan and Nazi terror campaigns against Black families in the West Englewood section of Chicago and in the Rosedale section of Queens, New York.

It is a question of groups that have carried out hundreds of lynchings of Blacks, and who often endorse Hitler's mass murder of the Jews and use of gangs of thugs with knives, blackjacks, and guns against trade unionists.

To call for banning or disrupting the racists' meetings shifts the axis of the struggle away from exposing their real nature as violent elements out to *attack* the democratic rights of working people and Blacks, and onto the question of whether *they* should have democratic rights.

The "no platform" tactic gives the racists and fascists a new weapon to use against their opponents. It allows these thugs to pose as a persecuted minority or as defenders of democratic rights.

Students, as well as most Americans, are correctly concerned about protecting their own democratic rights. The "no platform" position raises the question: Exactly which groups should be banned from expressing their views, and who is to decide this?

Where should the line be drawn? Should only open fascists be banned? What about the KKK, which does not claim to be fascist? What about racist groups like ROAR, in which fascists are active? What about less blatant but more powerful racists like President Ford, who gave the green light to the racist mobs in Boston with his statement against busing last fall? What about Boston Mayor Kevin White, who has made secret deals with ROAR and promised them money out of city funds? What about the notorious racist George Meany?

The confusion is confounded by the fact that some of the sectarian groups that call for "no platform for fascists" have their own definition of "fascists." For example, the Revolutionary Student Brigade calls the YSA "fascist" and has physically attacked YSA members selling the *Young Socialist* and the *Militant* in public places.

Some of these groups also include Democrats and Republicans in their category of who should not be allowed to speak publicly. The Progressive Labor party and the Spartacist League, among other groups, tried numerous times to shout down Democratic party politicians who spoke at antiwar meetings and demonstrations in the 1960s and early 1970s.

This "no platform" approach generates fear of radicals as small groups that are trying to force people to adhere to their views or be silent.

Many students and others can become so confused by these considerations that they will side with the racists on the question of free speech instead of joining antiracists in a counterdemonstration. Many of the people might be staunchly opposed to the racists and could contribute important forces to the struggle, if the tactics proposed did not confuse the issue.

It is useful to look further at the logic of the "no platform" position. Consider a hypothetical situation of a referendum on a campus to ban all racist speakers. One thing that could happen is that Zionist students—who have considerable strength on many campuses—could attempt to use such a ban against supporters of the Palestinian people. If it were agreed that a referendum could be used to ban racist ideas—and the ideas of the Zionists definitely fit that category—this could open the door to pro-Zionist student bodies voting to bar Arab speakers from the campus with the false charge that they are "anti-Semitic."

The concept of stamping out unpopular ideas—even by majority vote—clearly leads to more harm than good. Its logic is that only those ideas considered acceptable by the majority could be freely expressed—which automatically eliminates most radical ideas at present.

Students and faculty should be able to control the university facilities, but *not* what ideas can be expressed on campus. Democratic procedures imply not only majority rule, but also the right of free competition of ideas, on the basis of which people then make up their minds.

Just as antiracists should not call on the administration to ban fascist or racist speakers, it is also counterproductive to call on the university to fire racist professors simply because of their ideas. To do so would give the administration a chance to, as Malcolm X put it, make the criminal look like the victim and the victims look like the criminal.

The firing of professors with racist theories would set the precedent for the firing of Marxist or other radical professors. The authorities are always looking for excuses to fire dissident teachers—as happened to professors Angela Davis, Bruce Franklin, and Morris Starsky, to cite a few examples.

Of course, teachers who insult or mistreat their students in a racist manner, or are engaged in using campus facilities for police training, behavior modification, or other racist projects are a different question. There it is not a question of expression of ideas, but rather of the misuse of campus facilities for racist actions.

Another example that helps clarify this question is the struggle against military recruiters, ROTC (Reserve Officers Training Corps), and war research on campus. When this became an issue during the anti-Vietnam War movement, the YSA drew the distinction between a prowar speaker—such as Melvin Laird or William Westmoreland—and recruiters or researchers who were on campus to build up the war machine.

On the one hand, we did not try to bar prowar speakers because of their ideas. We helped organize demonstrations, picket lines, and sometimes debates. In this way we helped expose the prowar speaker as well as the federal government and any university complicity with the war.

But when military recruiters came onto campus, we demanded that the university withdraw its invitation to them. What was involved was not a question of democratic rights, but rather an attempt by the government to use campus facilities to help carry out their imperialist war effort in Vietnam.

Our opposition to ROTC and war research also stemmed from our view that the university should not be used as an arm of the military. In cases where the question was put to a referendum, the YSA and other antiwar students went on a campaign to convince the majority why ROTC should be thrown off campus.

These examples illustrate why an effective struggle against reactionary ideas and violence cannot be carried out if one begins by placing qualifications on democratic rights in the case of fascists.

This stand not only cuts across the mobilization of the maximum number of antiracist forces; it also reflects a lack of understanding of the prime importance of the principle of democratic rights to the working class and all the oppressed.

Democratic rights create better conditions for the education and organization of the oppressed against their oppressors. They mean the right to form trade unions and other organizations to defend the interests of the masses. They mean the right to hold meetings and distribute leaflets and newspapers, which is necessary for winning the majority away from the reactionaries.

Revolutionary socialists are for the fullest democratic rights under capitalism as well as under socialism. The only exception, in which a temporary abridgement of democratic rights might be called for, would be under conditions of civil war, when the logic of war becomes applicable.

One historical example that could be cited is the situation during the American Civil War. This war took place at a time when the capitalist system was still capable of carrying out a progressive fight against the more backward social system of slavery.

During the war, President Lincoln ordered that any person could be arrested in the North simply for speaking out in support of the Southern slaveholders. This was a violation of free speech, yet justified under conditions of warfare, when the Southern slaveowners had tried to violently frustrate the will of the majority in the country.

Likewise, during the Russian revolution of 1917 and after its victory, when twenty-two countries joined in military action to try to overthrow the first workers state, the Soviets banned those parties that joined forces with the counterrevolutionary side in the civil war.

Trotsky explained this in the following way in his article "Freedom of the Press and the Working Class" (*International Socialist Review*, June 1975): "Once at the helm, the proletariat may find itself forced, for a certain time, to take special measures against the bourgeoisie, if the bourgeoisie assumes an attitude of open rebellion against the workers state. In that case, restricting freedom of the press goes hand in hand with all the other measures employed in waging a civil war. Naturally, if you are forced to use artillery and planes against the enemy, you cannot permit this same enemy to maintain his own centers of news and propaganda within the armed camp of the proletariat."

Nevertheless, Trotsky warned that "measures of this kind can only be a temporary, unavoidable evil."

Because of the importance of democratic rights to the oppressed, the denial of this right to racists or fascists can only backfire. It has been proven throughout the history of capitalism that any suppression of democratic rights is ultimately turned against the working class.

One illustration of this is the application of the Smith Act, which supposedly banned "subversive" ideas from either the right or the left. While the thirty fascists indicted under this act during World War II got off scot-free, members of the Socialist Workers party and, after the war, the Communist party were convicted and given heavy prison sentences.

Another case where this problem was raised concerned a rally organized by George Lincoln Rockwell, former head of the American Nazis, for July 4, 1960, in New York City's Union Square. After a counterdemonstration against the Nazis was announced, the Nazis were denied a permit for the rally by the city government on the grounds that it might start a "riot."

The Socialist Workers party opposed this move by the city. It was clear that if the government was able to ban a fascist rally, it could do the same thing if the SWP or another workers organization or Black organization tried to organize a rally. The city government could use the same pretense—to prevent "riots" and "stop the extremists from both right and left."

At the same time, the SWP was in the forefront of organizing the counterdemonstration against the Nazis.

To call on the government or campus authorities to ban racist or fascist speakers helps to foster the illusion that the capitalist government and institutions can be looked to as a force to stop the fascists. History has shown, to the contrary, that the capitalist authorities, while claiming to stand for democracy, protect the reactionary terror gangs and look on them as the nuclei of the last-ditch defenders of their system.

As Leon Trotsky explained in his article "Why I Consented to Appear Before the Dies Committee": "The outlawing of fascist groups would inevitably have a fictitious character: as reactionary organizations they can easily change color and adapt themselves to any kind of organizational form since the influential sections of the ruling class and of the governmental apparatus sympathize considerably with them and these sympathies inevitably increase during times of political crisis."

While opposing government denial of free speech and assembly to anyone, the antiracist forces should vigorously call for government arrest and prosecution of racists or right-wingers who carry out any acts of violence.

A call for the arrest of rightist terrorists is not a call on the government to restrict democratic rights, but rather to *enforce* the democratic right of everyone to equal protection of the law against physical attack.

Here again there is the problem that the capitalist government does not consistently defend democratic rights. The government and its police will drag their feet on taking any action against rightist thugs. But a campaign exposing their protection of rightist hoodlums can force them to take some action.

The best current example of this kind of campaign is in Los Angeles, where the Nazis and Cuban counterrevolutionary gangs have carried out a series of terror bombings and arson against the YSA, the SWP, and other groups. There the YSA's approach is to focus on forcing the city government, headed by Mayor Tom Bradley, to arrest and prosecute those responsible, and building mass support for our democratic right to exist, through united-front protests with all those concerned about this terrorist threat.

The YSA does not, however, call on the government to ban the Nazis, nor do we propose that Nazis be prohibited from speaking on campuses in the city.

Another argument used to justify a call for banning or physically breaking up reactionary meetings is that fascism can thereby be "nipped in the bud," or somehow stopped even before it gets started.

For example, the *Young Spartacus*, publication of the SYL, carried an article in its June 1975 issue that prominently displayed in large letters a quote attributed to the German fascist leader Joseph Goebbels: "If the enemy had known how weak we were, it would probably have reduced us to jelly. . . . It would have crushed in blood the very beginning of our work." The implication is that that is precisely what should be done today. And the method, the article explains, is to do as the Young Spartacus League did March 10 at San Francisco State University. The SYL and others physically attacked a few fascists scheduled to speak in a class on campus. Their slogan was "No platform for fascists."

All this succeeded in doing was to give the Nazis the opportunity to return to the campus with leaflets protesting the denial of their democratic rights, while making the Spartacus Youth League look like it was against democratic rights.

Such tactics reinforce the prejudices of many people who think socialists are fighting for a system that will do away with democratic rights, as is the case in the Soviet Union. To the contrary, socialists must convince the masses of people that they are the most consistent defenders of democratic rights, against the government's infringement of those rights.

The SYL tactics cut across the main axis of the fight against the fascists: their threat to the democratic rights of others. The task for socialists is not to prove their "toughness" in fighting handfuls of fascists, but rather to build an effective mass response that isolates and demoralizes them.

A fascist movement cannot be "nipped in the bud" no matter how many of their meetings are disrupted. This theory shows a lack of understanding of the social conditions and forces that lie behind the growth of fascist organizations.

The development of a real fascist threat will not be the work of the handful of individuals who make up the fascist groups today. It will be a mass movement playing on the fears of large sections of the population and backed by major sectors of the ruling class. The despair created by economic crisis, together with the aid and comfort provided to fascist demagogues by the ruling class, will bring forth new fascist forces no matter how many individual rightists are beaten up by the tiny SYL today. They can only be defeated by the conscious action of masses of working people and Black people who have learned through their own experience what they represent.

In their frenzy to "nip the fascists in the bud," the SYL and other ultraleft groups fail to see the greater challenge posed today by groups such as ROAR, or the racists Jensen and Shockley. This was obvious in an article in the May 23 issue of *Workers Vanguard*, newspaper of the Spartacist League, describing an incident along the line of march at the May 17 antiracist demonstration in Boston.

"The marchers' response to a small counterdemonstration by a band of Nazis was instructive," says the article. "As the SL and others moved to deal with the racist scum, SWP and NAACP marchers linked arms to keep the indignant crowd from getting at the Fascists. The police moved immediately to protect the Nazis."

The demonstration marshals were completely right to try to avoid provocations from the group of Nazis and halt the irresponsible actions of the SL in order to keep the focus of the march clearly on ROAR and the Boston School Committee. A fracas with the Nazis could have given the cops an excuse to attack the whole demonstration.

In considering how to respond to reactionary speakers on campus, it is important to draw the distinction between racist forces such as Jensen and Shockley and ROAR on the one hand, and groups such as the American Nazis on the other. The Jensens and ROARs are not looked on by masses of Americans as the reactionaries they are. They are not seen as a threat to the whole working class. All too many white people even share their blatant prejudices.

The Nazis, on the other hand, are widely viewed as dangerous, or even "un-American."

The Jensens and the ROARs are the main threat today. They are the ones who are spearheading the government's racist offensive, which is affecting the entire Black community with discriminatory layoffs and cutbacks. Their racist theories of Black inferiority and their demand for racial segregation of schools gain a sympathetic response from millions of whites. Their demagogy must be seriously answered and exposed before the mass of students and of American working people.

If a ROAR representative comes onto a campus to speak, the antiracist forces should not call on the administration to ban the speaker. This would only provide ROAR and other racists with a phony "free speech" issue to aid them in their organizing efforts. More effective methods might be to challenge the racist speaker to a debate, to write leaflets and articles exposing their positions or to build a protest action with the broadest support possible.

The YSA has no disagreement with the proponents of the "no platform" approach that the racists and fascists on the rise today are vicious and dangerous scum. The disagreement is over *how* to combat them most effectively.

Most effective is to confront the fascists' ideas ideologically and their actions through counteractions.

The "no platform" approach blunts our effectiveness. It means that the struggle against racism and fascism is turned "inside out." Instead of coming across for what it really is—a struggle in defense of the democratic rights of the working class and oppressed minorities—the struggle is turned into a sterile dispute over the "rights" of the fascists. That is advantageous to them, not to the antiracist movement.

APPENDIX A: SELECTIONS FROM THE WRITINGS OF TROTSKY

The danger of ultraleft tactics in fighting fascists

The following letter, dated March 2, 1934, was addressed by Leon Trotsky to his followers in France. It is printed by permission of Pathfinder Press from a forthcoming volume of the series *Writings of Leon Trotsky (1929–40)*. (Copyright 1975 by Pathfinder Press, Inc.) The translation from French is by Russell Block for Pathfinder Press.

Dear Friends,

Since I am in Switzerland,[1] I cannot follow the events in France at close hand. But let me say that before emigrating here, I accumulated a certain amount of experience in these matters in Germany. And the Menilmontant affair[2] fills me with the direst foreboding. If things proceed along this line, catastrophe is inevitable.

What is the objective, not just for the moment but for the entire coming period? It is to get the workers to take up the struggle against the fascists before these elements have become the dominant force in the state, to get the workers used to not being afraid of the fascists, to teach them how to deal blows to the fascists, to convince them that they are stronger in numbers, in audacity, and in other ways.

In this period it is very important to distinguish between the fascists and the state. The state is not yet ready to subordinate itself to the fascists; it wants to "arbitrate." We know what this means from the sociological point of view. However, this is not a matter of sociology but of giving blows and taking them. Politically it is part of the nature of a pre-Bonapartist, "arbiter" state that the police hesitate, hold back, and on the whole are far from identifying with the fascist gangs. Our strategic task is to increase these hesitations and apprehensions on the part of the "arbiter," its army and its police. How? By showing that we are stronger than the fascists, that is, by giving them a good beating in full view of this arbiter without, as long as we are not absolutely forced to, directly taking on the state itself. That is the whole point.

In the case of Menilmontant, as far as I can tell from here, the operation was handled in the diametrically opposite way. *L'Humanité* reports that there were no more than sixty fascists in a thoroughly working-class neighborhood! The tactical, or if you will, "technical," task was quite simple—grab every fascist or every isolated group of fascists by their collars, acquaint them with the pavement a few times, strip them of their fascist insignia and documents, and without carrying things any further, leave them with their fright and a few good black and blue marks.

The "arbiter" defended freedom of assembly (for the moment the state is also defending workers' meetings from the fascists). This being the case, it was totally idiotic to want to provoke an armed

---

Reprinted from the December 2, 1974 issue of *Intercontinental Press*.

1. The phrase "I am in Switzerland" is intended to help hide the author's identity. Actually Trotsky was living incognito in Barbizon, a village near Paris. Because of the pressure of the French authorities and threats emanating from both fascist and Stalinist circles, he could not take a public stand on subjects as sensitive as the one he discusses here. In view of these conditions, Trotsky did not sign the letter.

2. For material on the Menilmontant affair, see "Background to Trotsky's Letter on Tactics in Fighting Fascists" by Gerry Foley, which appears elsewhere in this issue of *Intercontinental Press*.

conflict with the police. But this is precisely what they did. *L'Humanité* is exultant—they erected a barricade! But what for? The fascists weren't on the other side of the barricade, and it was the fascists they came to fight. Was this an armed insurrection, perhaps? To establish the dictatorship of the proletariat in Menilmontant? This makes no sense. As Marx said, "One does not play at insurrection." That means, "One does not play with barricades." Even when there is an insurrection, you don't erect barricades just anywhere, any time. (You can learn something from Blanqui on this score—see the documents published in *La Critique Sociale*.)[3]

They succeeded in (a) letting the gilded youth[4] return home in fine shape; (b) provoking the police and getting a worker killed; (c) giving the fascists an important argument—the Communists are starting to build barricades.

The idiot bureaucrats will say: "So, you want us to forget about building barricades out of fear of the Fascists and love of the police?" It is a betrayal to reject building barricades when the political situation demands it and when you are strong enough to erect them and defend them. But it is a disgusting provocation to build sham barricades for a little fascist meeting, to blow things up out of all political proportions, and to disorient the proletariat.

The task is to *involve* the workers in increasing numbers in the fight against fascism. The Menilmontant adventure can only isolate a small, militant minority. After such an experience, a hundred, a thousand workers who would have been ready to teach the young bourgeois bullies a few lessons will say, "No thanks, I don't want to get my head broken for nothing." The upshot of the whole undertaking was just the opposite of what was intended. And not to mince words, it wouldn't surprise me very much if it came out after a while that the ones who shouted loudest for the barricades were fascist agents planted in the ranks of the Stalinists, fascists who wanted to get their friends off the hook by provoking a confrontation with the police. If this was the case, they succeeded well.

What should the most active and perceptive elements have done on the spot? They should have improvised a small general staff, including a socialist and a Stalinist if possible. (At the same time it should have been explained to the workers that the neighborhood general staff should have functioned on a permanent basis on the eve of the demonstration.) This improvised general staff, with a map of the district spread out in front of them, should have worked out the simplest plan in the world—divide up one or two hundred demonstrators into groups of three to five, with a leader for each group, and let them do their work. And after the battle the leaders should get together and draw the balance sheet and the necessary lessons for the future. This second meeting could provide a good core for a permanent general staff, a good underpinning for a permanent workers militia in the district. Naturally, there would have to be leaflets explaining the need for a permanent general staff.

For the perceptive, revolutionary elements, the balance sheet offers the following lessons:

a. You have to have your own general staff for such occasions.

b. You have to anticipate the possibilities and eventualities in such conflicts.

c. You have to establish a few general plans (several variants).

d. You have to have a map of the district.

e. You have to have the proper leaflets for the situation.

This is all I can say for the moment. I am almost sure that these suggestions are completely in accord with your own ideas. So much the better.

---

3. Louis-Auguste Blanqui (1805–81) was one of the great revolutionists of the French working class. The Critique Sociale (Social Criticism), a collection of his writings, was published in 1885. Blanqui spent almost half his life in prison—thirty-seven years—because of repeated participation in the armed action of small groups. Engels in 1874 said of him: "Blanqui is really a political revolutionary, socialist only in his emotions, sympathising with the sufferings of the people, but without a social theory of definite, practical proposals for social reform; in his political action he is essentially a man of deeds, and is of the opinion that a small, well-organised minority, which strikes at the right moment, can carry with it the mass of the population and thus consummate a successful revolution. One sees that Blanqui is the revolutionary of a past generation."

4. "Gilded youth." Youths of wealthy background who sought excitement, including violence, in ultrareactionary movements. Until recent years, it was quite rare for youths of well-to-do families to find their way to the cause of the proletariat. References to the "gilded youth" and their readiness to play the role of "young bourgeois bullies" can be found in socialist literature going back to the 1840s.

Background to Trotsky's letter on tactics in fighting fascists
By Gerry Foley

"An Unheard of Provocation," the headline said in the February 26, 1934, issue of the French Communist party organ *l'Humanité*, "They Are Holding a Fascist Meeting Tonight in the Twentieth Arrondissement of Paris! The Twentieth Section of the Socialist Party Rejects a United Front of Action. Workers Strike Back Under the Leadership of the CP!"

The meeting in question was a rally in the Twentieth Arrondissement staged by "national groups"—the Action Française, the Jeunesses Patriotes (Patriotic Youth), Solidarité Française, the Federation des Contribuables (Taxpayers Federation) and others. It was to be held in the Salon des Prévoyants on the Rue des Pyrénées, in the center of the working-class Menilmontant district.

The Communist party's appeal for an antifascist action under its own banner, coupled with a denunciation of other working-class organizations for not participating, was typical of the ultraleft phase of Stalinism from 1928 to 1934.

The Comintern said that the world had entered the "Third Period," the period of the final and inevitably fatal crisis of capitalism.

Its concept of the "united front from below" was a corollary of this notion. Since revolution was on the immediate agenda, the primary obstacle was the reformist forces in the workers movement. But, in view of the momentum of the revolutionary crisis, the CPs could simply ride over them.

In the period following the Nazi victory in Germany, which was facilitated by the ultraleftist aberrations of the Comintern and the German CP, the Kremlin made a complete about-face. It began calling for a "Popular Front" with the bourgeois parliamentary parties that represented the same fundamental class interests as the fascists and that were bowing to fascism wherever capitalism was threatened.

The shift had a certain logic. It was, in fact, just the other side of the coin of ultraleftism. Whereas the bureaucracy had hoped before to override the basic social laws by using its "muscle," now it was trying to do the same thing by diplomatic deals with sections of the ruling class.

Even after the Nazi victory in Germany, it took Stalin some time to decide to change the line. It was only in June 1934, for instance, that the French Communist party formally proclaimed the turn to "unity against fascism."

However, on February 6, 1934, the fascists had already come within an inch of taking power in the country during the Stavisky riots. It was fortunate that the capitalist class did not yet feel the need to rely on the fascists to "restore order." The police of the Daladier government fired on the fascist demonstrators and forced them to retreat.

Trapped by its ultraleft line, the Communist party was unable to respond to the fascist threat by projecting a line to mobilize the masses. In fact, it joined the fascist demonstrations of February 6, later echoing the fascist complaints about police "gunslingers," apparently on the theory that since revolution was immediately on the agenda any challenge to the institutions of bourgeois legality opened the way for war on the capitalist state.

The fascist take-over attempt sparked a tremendous upsurge among the workers. The Communist party itself was swept along for a moment despite its sectarian line. At the last minute, it made a quick switch, coming out in support of the call for a nationwide one-day general strike on February 12, which turned into a massive demonstration of the potential power of the working class.

The development of these united mass actions by the workers was a resounding confirmation of the line put forward by the small French Trotskyist organization, the Ligue Communiste (Communist League).

"Everywhere the Ligue had a nucleus or even an isolated activist," a participant recalled, "workers alliance committees sprang up. This was the case in Suresnes, Boulogne, and Corbeil, where these committees included *organizations* determined to struggle. In the provinces the Trotskyists were in the forefront of the street demonstrations. The power of their slogans was such that they were acclaimed at the Socialist party rally in Wagram, and for the first time a representative of theirs was able to speak—for ten minutes—at the big Communist rally in Bullier."[1]

However, this upsurge did not convince the CP of the need for united class action. Paradoxically, it may even have prolonged the plausibility of the Third Period line. Schooled in ultraleftism and get-rich-quick schemes, the CP cadres could have thought that now only a spark was needed to ignite a prairie fire.

In the first phase of an upsurge, the bankruptcy of ultraleftism is not as apparent as it is in quieter times, or at the decisive moment. Ultraleft initiatives can feed on the general radicalization and appeal in particular to the impatient. It is precisely in such phases, on the other hand, that ultraleftism presents its greatest dangers by threatening to disorient and destroy the most advanced and courageous elements and scatter rather than assemble the forces needed to win a decisive victory over capitalism.

The Menilmontant operation was a good example of such an ultraleft adventure:

"The assassins of the workers intend to use their strength to burn our district," the February 26 l'Humanité article declared.

"In spite of this threat, a leader of the Twentieth Section of the Socialist party has refused to discuss organizing a counterdemonstration jointly with the Communists.

"But the Socialist party workers of the Twentieth Arrondissement recognize the danger of this massive fascist onslaught and will once again join in a united front in action with the Communists, as they have already many times in this struggle. *They will chase the fascists from the Twentieth!*"

This type of argument was hardly calculated to convince the Socialist party that the CP was really interested in united action; it put no pressure on the SP leaders either, since such appeals could easily be dismissed as arrogant Communist ultimatums or maneuvers.

The tactic that flowed from the conception of a "united front from below" aimed at drawing the Socialist party rank and file in behind the initiatives of the Communist party, by sheer momentum and force of example. Although the CP did engage in some negotiations for united action, they were subordinated to this perspective.

For example, the February 27 l'Humanité reported that three delegates from the SP Twentieth District had met with CP representatives before the demonstration of February 26 and that a common leaflet had been drawn up. There had, however, been no time to report this in the issue of the paper calling the action. Thus it was the CP's initiative that was held to be important, the example of "someone" attacking the fascists, not the achievement of working-class unity against the fascist threat.

This fact was shown clearly in the character of the demonstration. The action was a "propaganda" success, as the ultraleft CP saw it.

"The [fascist] meeting was small," the February 27 l'Humanité report continued. "Some sixty members of the JP, Croix de Feu, Solidarité Française, etc., dared venture into the meeting under the protection of more than 400 police who blocked the streets.

"But in spite of the masses of police protecting the fascists, the demonstration began at 8:30.

"One group began to demonstrate at Rue Vitruve. Another in the Rue Bagnolet facing the Brasserie George [the fascist meeting was transferred there], where the windows were broken. Meanwhile another group demonstrated on the other side of the café on the Rue de Pyrénées. The 2,000 demonstrators raised powerful chants: 'Soviets everywhere!' 'Unity in action!' 'Down with fascism!' 'Jail Tardieu!'

"The police tried to cut off the demonstrators, but they managed to mount an assault on the fascist meeting place for an hour and a half.

"Around 9:30 a new column of 400 to 500 demonstrators marched toward the brasserie. They were driven back by a police charge, but they returned.

"At 10:30, protected by the masses of cops, the five or six dozen fascists began to leave two by two, after putting out the lights. Many were recognized and taught a lesson by the workers.

"It was a rout!

"The demonstration had attained a magnificent breadth.

"Toward 10 there was a rally of workers around La Bellevoise. A column of a thousand workers

---

1. Yvan Craipeau, *Le mouvement Trotskyste en France: Des origines aux enseignements de mai 68*, Editions Syros, Paris, 1971, pp. 95–96.

marched down the Rue Menilmontant. At the intersection of Rue Panoyaux, two carloads of police charged into the crowd. There was a fight.

"Immediately the crowd took boards from a local market and built many barricades. A police car drove up. The workers welcomed it with a hail of stones. The car was forced to drive behind a barricade to escape.

"A police car coming from the direction of the Courronne metro station was received in turn with a shower of stones thrown by the workers behind the barricades. For many minutes, the workers battled the cops, pushing them back behind their car, and then more rocks were thrown. At this moment five shots from a revolver were fired at the workers. We have learned that one comrade has been grievously wounded by a shot in the head.

"Another comrade was wounded in the stomach, and two others were also hit. . . ."

The February 28 *l'Humanite* gave more details. A 19-year-old construction worker, H. Wilhemin, was killed. But his funeral was another even more successful demonstration of "unity in action."

"There were 80,000 of us behind Wilhemin's coffin. From Belleville of the barricades to the Pantin Parmila cemetery there was a chorus of fraternal rage, a hundred thousand fists raised. . . .

"'We will avenge you, comrade.' 'The cops are murderers!' 'Jail the head cop Chiappe!' 'The soldiers are with us!' 'Down with Laval-Tardieu!' '*Soviets everywhere!*'"

This action was another clear example of the ultraleft course Leon Trotsky had campaigned against in the case of Germany.

From 'The death agony of capitalism and the tasks of the Fourth International'

Reprinted by permission. The following is an excerpt from the "Transitional Program," the main resolution adopted by the founding congress of the Fourth International in 1938. It is reprinted from *The Transitional Program for Socialist Revolution* (New York: Pathfinder, 1974). It is © 1974 by Pathfinder Press, Inc.

The picket line/defense guards/workers' militia/the arming of the proletariat

Sit-down strikes are a serious warning from the masses addressed not only to the bourgeoisie but also to the organizations of the workers, including the Fourth International. In 1919–20, the Italian workers seized factories on their own initiative, thus signaling the news to their "leaders" of the coming of the social revolution. The "leaders" paid no heed to the signal. The victory of fascism was the result.

Sit-down strikes do not yet mean the seizure of factories in the Italian manner; but they are a decisive step toward such seizures. The present crisis can sharpen the class struggle to an extreme point and bring nearer the moment of denouement. But that does not mean that a revolutionary situation comes on at one stroke. Actually, its approach is signalized by a continuous series of convulsions. One of these is the wave of sit-down strikes. The problem of the sections of the Fourth International is to help the proletarian vanguard understand the general character and tempo of our epoch and to fructify in time the struggle of the masses with ever more resolute and militant organizational measures.

The sharpening of the proletariat's struggle means the sharpening of the methods of counterattack on the part of capital. New waves of sit-down strikes can call forth and undoubtedly will call forth resolute countermeasures on the part of the bourgeoisie. Preparatory work is already being done by the confidential staffs of big trusts. Woe to the revolutionary organizations, woe to the proletariat if it is again caught unawares!

The bourgeoisie is nowhere satisfied with official police and army. In the United States, even during "peaceful" times, the bourgeoisie maintains militarized battalions of scabs and privately armed thugs in factories. To this must now be added the various groups of American Nazis. The French bourgeoisie at the first approach of danger mobilized semilegal and illegal fascist detachments, including such as are in the army. No sooner does the pressure of the English workers once again become stronger than immediately the fascist bands are doubled, trebled, increased tenfold to come out in bloody march against the workers. The bourgeoisie keeps itself most accurately informed about the fact that in the present epoch the class struggle irresistibly tends to transform itself into civil war. The examples of Italy, Germany, Austria, Spain, and other countries taught considerably more to the magnates and lackeys of capital than to the official leaders of the proletariat.

The politicians of the Second and Third Internationals, as well as the bureaucrats of the trade unions, consciously close their eyes to the bourgeoisie's private army; otherwise, they could not preserve their alliance with it for even twenty-four hours. The reformists systematically implant in the minds of the workers the notion that the sacredness of democracy is best guaranteed when the bourgeoisie is armed to the teeth and the workers are unarmed.

The duty of the Fourth International is to put an end to such slavish politics once and for all. The petty-bourgeois democrats—including Social Democrats, Stalinists, and Anarchists—yell louder about the struggle against fascism the more cravenly they capitulate to it in actuality. Only armed workers' detachments, who feel the support of tens of millions of toilers behind them, can successfully prevail against the fascist bands. The struggle against fascism does not start in the liberal editorial office but in the factory—and ends in the street. Scabs and private gunmen in factory plants are the basic nuclei of the fascist army. *Strike pickets* are the basic nuclei of the proletarian army. This is our point of departure. In connection with every strike and street demonstration, it is imperative to propagate the necessity of creating *workers' groups for self-defense*. It is necessary to write this slogan into the program of the revolutionary wing of the trade unions. It is imperative wherever possible, beginning with the youth groups, to organize groups for self-defense, to drill and acquaint them with the use of arms.

A new upsurge of the mass movement should serve not only to increase the number of these units but also to unite them according to neighborhoods, cities, regions. It is necessary to give organized expression to the valid hatred of the workers toward scabs and bands of gangsters and fascists. It is necessary to advance the slogan of a *workers' militia* as the one serious guarantee for the inviolability of workers' organizations, meetings, and press.

Only with the help of such systematic, persistent, indefatigable, courageous agitational and organizational work, always on the basis of the experience of the masses themselves, is it possible to root out from their consciousness the traditions of submissiveness and passivity; to train detachments of heroic fighters capable of setting an example to all toilers; to inflict a series of tactical defeats upon the armed thugs of counterrevolution; to raise the self-confidence of the exploited and oppressed; to compromise fascism in the eyes of the petty bourgeoisie and pave the road for the conquest of power by the proletariat.

Engels defined the state as bodies of "armed men." *The arming of the proletariat* is an imperative concomitant element to its struggle for liberation. When the proletariat wills it, it will find the road and the means to arming. In this field, also, the leadership falls naturally to the sections of the Fourth International.

From 'Why I consented to appear before the Dies Committee'

Reprinted by permission. The following article, written on March 11, 1939, first appeared in the December 30, 1939, issue of Socialist Appeal. It is reprinted from Writings of Leon Trotsky [1939–40] (New York: Pathfinder, 1973). The Dies Committee was the House Un-American Activities Committee headed by Texas Democrat Martin Dies. It is © 1973 by Pathfinder Press, Inc.

Why did I agree to appear before the Dies Committee? Naturally not in order to facilitate the realization of Mr. Dies's political aims, particularly the passing of federal laws against one or another extremist "party." Being an irreconcilable opponent not only of fascism but also of the present-day Comintern, I am at the same time decidedly against the suppression of either of them.

The outlawing of fascist groups would inevitably have a fictitious character: as reactionary organizations they can easily change color and adapt themselves to any kind of organizational form since the influential sections of the ruling class and of the governmental apparatus sympathize considerably with them and these sympathies inevitably increase during times of political crisis.

As for the Comintern, suppression could only help this completely degenerated and compromised organization. The difficulty in the Comintern's situation is a result of the irreconcilable contradiction between the international workers' movement and the interests of the Kremlin ruling clique. After all its zigzags and deceptions, the Comintern has obviously entered its period of decomposition. The suppression of the Communist Party would immediately re-establish its reputation in the eyes of the workers as a persecuted fighter against the ruling classes.

However, the question is not exhausted by this consideration. Under the conditions of the bourgeois regime, all suppression of political rights and freedom, no matter whom they are directed against in the beginning, in the end inevitably bear down upon the working class, particularly its most advanced elements. That is a law of history. The workers must learn how to distinguish between their friends and their enemies according to their own judgment and not according to the hints of the police.

It is not difficult to predict an ad hominem objection: "But just that Soviet government in which you yourself took part proscribed all political parties except the Bolsheviks?" Entirely correct; and to this day I am ready to bear responsibility for its actions. But one cannot identify the laws of civil war with the laws of peaceful periods; the laws of the dictatorship of the proletariat with the laws of bourgeois democracy.

If one considered Abraham Lincoln's policy exclusively from the point of view of civil liberties, then the great president would not appear very favorably. In justification of course he could say that he was compelled to apply civil war measures in order to cleanse the democracy of slavery. Civil war is a state of tense social crisis. One or another dictatorship, inevitably growing out of the conditions of civil war, appears fundamentally as an exception to the rule, a temporary regime.

It is true that the dictatorship in the Soviet Union did not die out, but on the contrary took on monstrous totalitarian forms. This is explained by the fact that out of the revolution arose a new privileged caste which is incapable of maintaining its regime except through measures of a hidden civil war. It was precisely over this question that I broke with the Kremlin ruling clique. I was defeated because the working class, as a result of internal and external conditions, showed itself to be too weak to liquidate its own bureaucracy. I have, however, no doubt that the working class will liquidate it.

But whatever the situation in the USSR may be, the working class in the capitalist countries, threatened with their own enslavement, must stand in defense of freedom for all political tendencies including their own irreconcilable enemies. That is why I do not feel the slightest sympathy for the aims of the Dies Committee.

On the question of workers' self-defense (October 25, 1939)

Reprinted by permission. In this article, Trotsky discussed the perspectives for building workers' defense guards in the wake of the opening of World War II. It is reprinted from Writings of Leon Trotsky: [1939–40]. *It is © 1973 by Pathfinder Press.*

Every state is a coercive organization of the ruling class. The social regime remains stable so long as the ruling class is capable, by means of the state, of imposing its will on the exploited classes. The police and the army are the most important instruments of the state. The capitalists refrain (though not fully, by far) from maintaining their own private armies, declining in favor of the state, so as thus to hinder the working class from ever creating its own armed force.

While the capitalist system is on the rise, the state monopoly of the armed forces is perceived as something natural, even by the oppressed classes.

Before the last world war, the international Social Democracy, even in its best periods, did not even raise the question of arming the workers. What's more, they rejected such an idea as a romantic echo of the remote past.

It was only in czarist Russia that the young proletariat in the first years of this century began to resort to arming their own fighting detachments. This revealed the instability of the old regime in the most vivid fashion. The czarist monarchy found itself less and less able to regulate social relations by means of its normal agencies, i.e., the police and the army; and it was forced more and more to resort to the aid of volunteer bands (the Black Hundreds with their pogroms against the Jews, Armenians, students, workers, and others). In response to this the workers, as well as various nationality groups, began to organize their own self-defense detachments. These facts indicated the beginning of the revolution.

In Europe the question of armed workers' detachments arose only toward the end of the war; in the United States it arose even later. In all cases, without exception, it was and is the capitalist reaction that first begins to set up special fighting organizations, which exist side by side with the police and army of the bourgeois state. This is explained by the fact that the bourgeoisie is more farsighted and ruthless than the proletariat. Under the pressure of class contradictions, it no longer relies totally on its own state, since the state's hands are still tied to a certain extent by "democratic" norms. The appearance of "volunteer" fighting organizations that have as their objective the physical suppression of the proletariat is an unmistakable symptom that the disintegration of democracy has begun, owing to the fact that it is no longer possible to regulate the class contradictions by the old methods.

The hope of the reformist parties of the Second and Third Internationals and trade unions that the organs of the democratic state would defend them from fascist gangs has always and everywhere turned out to be an illusion. During serious crises, the police invariably maintain a posture of friendly neutrality, if not outright collaboration, with respect to the counterrevolutionary gangs. However, the extreme vitality of democratic illusions results in the workers being very slow to take up organizing their own fighting detachments. The designation "self-defense" fully corresponds to their intentions, at least in the first period, because the attack invariably originates from the side of the counterrevolutionary gangs. Monopoly capital, which is backing them up, launches a *preventive* war against the proletariat, in order to render it incapable of making a socialist revolution.

The process by which workers' self-defense detachments come into being is inseparably linked with the entire course of the class struggle in a country; and, therefore, reflects its inevitable aggravations and moderations, its ebbs and flows. Revolution comes upon a society not by a steady unbroken process, but through a series of convulsions, separated by distinct, sometimes protracted intervals, during which the political relations are so modified that the very idea of revolution seems to lose any connection with reality.

In accordance with this, the slogan of self-defense units at one time will meet a sympathetic response, and at another will sound like a voice calling in the wilderness, and then again, after a while, will acquire new popularity.

This contradictory process can be observed especially clearly in France over the course of recent years. As a result of a creeping economic crisis, reaction openly went over to the offensive in February 1934. Fascist organizations experienced rapid growth. On the other hand, the idea of self-defense acquired popularity in the ranks of the working class. Even the reformist Socialist Party in Paris was compelled to create something akin to a self-defense apparatus.

The "People's Front" policy, i.e., the complete prostration of the workers' organizations before the bourgeoisie, postponed the danger of revolution to the indefinite future and allowed the bourgeoisie to take the fascist coup off the agenda. Moreover, having been freed from immediate internal dangers and finding themselves face to face with an intensifying threat from abroad, the French bourgeoisie began immediately to exploit, for imperialist aims, the fact that democracy had been "saved."

The impending war was again proclaimed to be a war to preserve democracy. The politics of the official workers' organizations took on an openly imperialist character. The section of the Fourth International, having taken a serious step forward in 1934, felt isolated in the period that followed. The call for workers' self-defense hung in mid-air. Who in fact were they to defend themselves from? After all, "democracy" had triumphed all along the line. . . . The French bourgeoisie had entered this war under the banner of "democracy" and with the support of all the official workers' organizations, which permitted the "Radical Socialist" Daladier to immediately set up a "democratic" likeness of a totalitarian regime.

The question of self-defense organizations will be revived in the ranks of the French proletariat with the growth of revolutionary resistance against the war and imperialism. The subsequent political development of France, and of other countries as well, at the present time is inseparably linked with the war. The growth of mass discontent will at first give rise to the most savage reaction from above. Militarized fascism will come to the aid of the bourgeoisie and its state power. The issue of organization for self-defense will confront the working class as a life-and-death matter. This time, one must assume there will turn out to be a sufficient supply of rifles, machine-guns, and cannons in the hands of the working class.

Similar phenomena, although in less vivid form, were revealed in the political life of the United States. After the successes of the Roosevelt era, betraying all expectations, gave way in the autumn of 1937 to a headlong decline, reaction began to come forward in an open and militant manner. The provincial mayor Hague immediately became a "national" figure. The pogrom-minded sermons of Father Coughlin were echoed widely. The Democratic administration and its police retreated in the face of monopoly capital's gangs. In this period the idea of military detachments for the defense of the workers' organizations and press began to get a response among the most conscious workers and the most threatened stratum of the petty bourgeoisie, particularly among the Jews.

The new economic revival, which began in July 1939, obviously connected with armaments expansion and the imperialist war, revived the faith of the Sixty Families in their "democracy." To this was added on the other hand the danger of the United States being drawn into the war. This was no time to rock the boat! All the sections of the bourgeoisie closed ranks behind a policy of caution and preservation of "democracy." Roosevelt's position in Congress is becoming stronger. Hague and Father Coughlin have retired far into the background. Simultaneously the Dies Committee, which neither the right nor the left took seriously in 1937, has acquired in recent months considerable authority. The bourgeoisie is again "against fascism as well as communism"; it wants to show that it can cope with all types of "extremism" by parliamentary means.

Under these conditions, the slogan of workers' self-defense cannot help but lose its power of attraction. After an encouraging beginning it is as though the organizing of workers' self-defense has wound up at a dead end.

In some places it is difficult to draw the workers' attention to the matter. In others, where large numbers of workers have joined self-defense groups, the leaders don't know how to make use of the workers' energy. Interest wanes. There is nothing unexpected or puzzling about all this. The entire history of workers' self-defense organizations is one of constantly alternating periods of rise and decline. Both reflect spasms of the social crisis.

The tasks of the proletarian party in the area of workers' self-defense flow from the general conditions of our epoch as well as from its particular fluctuations. It is immeasurably easier to draw relatively broad sections of the working class into fighting detachments in circumstances when reactionary gangs are making direct attacks on workers' picket lines, trade unions, press, etc. However, when the bourgeoisie considers it more prudent to abandon the irregular bands and push methods of "democratic" domination over the masses into the foreground, the workers' interest in self-defense organizations inevitably diminishes. This is what is happening right now. Does this mean, however, that we should abandon the task of arming the workers' vanguard under these conditions?

Not at all. Now, at a time when the world war has begun, more than ever before, we proceed from the inevitability and imminence of the international proletarian revolution. This fundamental idea, which distinguishes the Fourth International from all other workers' organizations, determines all our activities, including those which relate to the organization of self-defense detachments. This does not mean, however, that we do not take into account the conjunctural fluctuations in the economy as well as in politics, with the temporary ebbs and flows. If one proceeds only on the basis of the overall characterization of the epoch, and nothing more, ignoring its concrete stages, one can easily lapse into schematism, sectarianism, or quixotic fantasy. With every serious turn of events we adjust our basic tasks to the changed concrete conditions of the given stage. Herein lies the art of tactics.

We will need party cadres specializing in military affairs. They must, therefore, continue their practical and theoretical work even now, in a time of "low tide." The theoretical work must consist of studying the experience of military and combat organizations of the Bolsheviks, the Irish and Polish revolutionary nationalists, the fascists, the Spanish militia, and others. We must put together a model program of studies and a library on these matters, arrange lectures, and so forth.

Staff work must at the same time be continued without interruption. We must assemble and study newspaper clippings and other information concerning every kind of counterrevolutionary organization and, at the same time, of national groupings (Jews, Negroes, and others), which in a critical moment can play a revolutionary role. This is, in fact, relevant to an extremely important part of our work, devoted to defense against the GPU.

Precisely on account of the exceptionally difficult situation into which the Comintern has fallen—and to a considerable extent the foreign GPU secret service which is supported by the Comintern—we can expect vicious blows at the Fourth International on the part of the GPU. We must be able to find them out and avert them in time!

Alongside this tightly restricted work, intended for party members only, we must create broader, open organizations for various kinds of particular objectives, one way or another connected to the future military tasks of the proletariat. This would pertain to various kinds of workers' sports organizations (for athletes, boxers, marksmen, etc.), and finally, choral and music societies. When there is a shift in the political situation, all these subsidiary organizations can serve as an immediate basis for broader detachments for workers' self-defense.

In this outline of a program for action we proceed from the view that the political conditions of the given moment, above all the weakening of the pressure of domestic fascism, leave narrow limits for work in the area of self-defense. And that is the case in so far as it is a matter of creating strictly class-based military detachments.

A decisive turn in favor of workers' self-defense will come only with a new collapse of democratic illusions, which under conditions of world war should come quickly and should assume catastrophic proportions.

But by way of compensation, the war is opening up now, at this very moment, such possibilities for the training of workers in military affairs as were impossible even to conceive of in peacetime. And this is true not only of the war but also of the period immediately preceding the war.

It is impossible to foresee all the practical possibilities beforehand; but they will undoubtedly become wider with each passing day as the country's armed forces expand. We must focus the greatest attention on this matter, creating a special commission for this purpose (or entrusting the matter to a self-defense staff and enlarging it as need be).

Most of all we must take full advantage of the interest in military problems which has been aroused by the war and organize a series of lectures on questions of contemporary arms types and tactical methods. Workers' organizations can enlist for this military specialists who have absolutely no ties to the party and its aims. But this is only the first step.

We must use the government's preparations for war in order to train in military matters the largest possible number of party members and trade unionists under its influence. While fully maintaining our fundamental aim—the creation of class-based military detachments—we must firmly link its accomplishment with the conditions created by the imperialists' preparations for war.

Without in any way wavering from our program we must speak to the masses in a language they understand. "We Bolsheviks also want to defend democracy, but not the kind that is run by sixty uncrowned kings. First let's sweep our democracy clean of capitalist magnates, then we will defend it to the last drop of blood. Are you, who are not Bolsheviks, really ready to defend *this* democracy? But you must, at least, be able to the best of your ability to defend it so as not to be a blind instrument in the hands of the Sixty Families and the bourgeois officers devoted to them. The working class must learn military affairs in order to advance the largest possible number of officers from its own ranks.

"We must demand that the state, which tomorrow will ask for the workers' blood, today give the workers the opportunity to master military technique in the best possible way in order to achieve the military objectives with the minimum expenditure of human lives.

"To accomplish that, a regular army and barracks by themselves are not enough. Workers must have the opportunity to get military training at their factories, plants, and mines at specified times, while being paid by the capitalists. If the workers are destined to give their lives, the bourgeois patriots can at least make a small material sacrifice.

"The state must issue a rifle to every worker capable of bearing arms and set up rifle and artillery ranges for military training purposes in places accessible to the workers."

Our agitation in connection with the war and all our politics connected with the war must be as uncompromising in relation to the pacifists as to the imperialists.

"This war is not our war. The responsibility for it lies squarely on the capitalists. But so long as we are still not strong enough to overthrow them and must fight in the ranks of their army, we are obliged to learn to use arms as well as possible!"

Women workers must also have the right to bear arms. The largest possible number of women workers must have the opportunity, at the capitalists' expense, to receive nurse's training.

Just as every worker, exploited by the capitalists, seeks to learn as well as possible the production techniques, so every proletarian soldier in the imperialist army must learn as well as possible the art of war so as to be able, when the conditions change, to apply it in the interests of the working class.

We are not pacifists. No. We are revolutionaries. And we know what lies ahead for us.

APPENDIX B: FROM 'THE CAPITALIST WITCH-HUNT —AND HOW TO FIGHT IT'

The following is an excerpt from a resolution adopted by the February 1950 plenum of the National Committee of the Socialist Workers Party. It is reprinted from the March–April 1950 issue of *Fourth International*, predecessor of the *International Socialist Review*.

Liberals, labor officials and the Stalinists often call upon the government and its agencies for action against ultra-reactionary elements. Jewish groups, for example, request the Post Office Department to ban anti-Semitic literature from the mails. Defaming the Trotskyists as agents of fascism, the Stalinists during the war demanded the suppression of *The Militant*, etc.

No dependence on capitalist state

The working class and the minorities must vigorously oppose every transgression upon their civil and constitutional rights, from whatever quarter they come, and utilize every safeguard provided by law. But they cannot entrust the protection of their liberties to the capitalist regime or expect the powers-that-be to stop or eradicate the menace of fascism.

First, the government itself today spearheads the assault upon the people's rights. The President orders the loyalty purge; Congress passes anti-labor legislation; the courts levy fines and issue injunctions against the unions. Second, the capitalist parties work hand in glove with white supremacists in the South and the Big Business enemies of labor in the North who are behind the witch-hunt.

Third, the authorities have time and again demonstrated by their action and inaction their lack of interest in punishing or removing the perpetrators of violence against the Negroes, the unions and the liberties of the people. Neither the Federal or State governments convict any lynchers in the South. Nor have the officials displayed much zeal in uncovering the murderous assailants of Carlo Tresca, William Lurye, the Reuthers, and other labor figures.

Government shields fascist elements

On the contrary, the capitalist state apparatus screens and shields fascist forces and collaborates closely with them. In Peekskill the local authorities and police connived in the attacks by the mobsters and hoodlums; Governor Dewey's investigators whitewashed their role; and the entire paid press tried to unload responsibility for the violence upon the "reds."

Even when, under pressure, government officials pretend to move against mobsters and Ku Kluxers, they only make theatrical gestures to appease outraged public opinion without actually punishing the real criminals. For every slight tap the capitalist agencies offer the right, they deliver a hundred harsh blows against the left. This has been illustrated by the Smith Act. While the 30 Fascists indicted under this Act in wartime were let off scot-free, the Trotskyists and Stalinists were convicted and given heavy jail sentences.

The same procedure has been followed in the loyalty purge. While the Attorney-General's blacklist includes a few fascist groups, in practice it is almost entirely applied against members of leftist organizations. The U.S. Department of Defense has given away the whole game by omitting the Ku Klux Klan, Silver Shirts and similar fascist outfits from its own subversive list applied to draftees.

"Under conditions of a capitalist regime," Trotsky once wrote, "all curtailment of political rights and freedoms, no matter against whom they may be originally directed, in the end inevitably fall with all their weight on the working class—especially on its most advanced elements."

How to fight fascism

Class-conscious workers should not fall into the trap of demanding infringements of anyone's civil rights, including those of the fascists. At the same time they should recognize the real situation and make it plain to others. The civil rights of fascist elements are not being threatened; the authorities are in league with them. They are in no danger of persecution or need of defense. They are not the victims but the sponsors and beneficiaries of the current repressions.

The menace of fascism does not arise from their propaganda but from their gangsterism, their mob attacks upon advanced workers, Negroes, and labor organizations. With tacit acquiescence of the authorities, the fascists operate as extralegal agencies of repression against the institutions and freedoms of the working class and minorities. Consequently, the real situation is that the labor organizations and minorities are obliged to act in self-defense to protect themselves against reactionary violence.

The history of Italy and Germany conclusively proves the folly and futility of relying upon the capitalist government, its police, or its parties in the fight against the fascists. The masses can safeguard their rights, their lives and their organizations only by mobilizing the full strength of their own forces in the most vigorous united and independent defensive actions against the race-bigots, anti-Semites, union-busters and mobsters who threaten them.

Organized labor has the ability as well as the duty to assume the leadership in this struggle. The trade unions are not only the chief bulwarks of democracy and the centers of proletarian power; they are likewise the main target of the capitalist authors of the witch-hunt whose ultimate objective is the destruction of the labor movement. The anti-labor campaign and anti-red hysteria are inseparable aspects of the monopolist drive toward the establishment of a police state in this country. Thus the defense of civil liberties is a life-and-death matter for American labor.

Without full democracy and freedom of expression inside the unions, they cannot effectively fulfill their tasks of defending the welfare of the workers and leading the struggle against reaction. Thus the fight for union democracy is directly interlinked with the general struggle for civil liberties.

APPENDIX C: AN EXAMPLE OF SECTARIAN ADVENTURISM IN THE STRUGGLE AGAINST FASCISM

Introductory note

Following are lengthy excerpts from two articles that originally appeared in *Young Spartacus*, a monthly newspaper published by the Spartacus Youth League (SYL). The SYL is an ultraleft sect, associated with the Spartacist League, that incorrectly describes itself as Trotskyist. Omissions from the original text are indicated by [. . .].

The articles deal with a March 10, 1975, demonstration organized by SYL for the explicit purpose of preventing a Nazi from speaking to a class at San Francisco State University. This action culminated in an unsuccessful administration effort to expel the SYL and other radical groups from the campus.

Underlying the demonstration was the concept that small groups of radicals should attempt to forestall the growth of a mass fascist movement by taking "upon themselves the suppression of fascist meetings and demonstrations," even if the surrounding community is hostile to the "suppression" and the working class is indifferent. SYL falsely asserts that this adventurist concept is rooted in the Transitional Program of the Fourth International.

The SYL justified its call for the suppression of free speech in this instance by arguing that, "Unlike right wing propaganda groups (John Birch Society), conservative bourgeois politicians (George Wallace) or reactionary academic ideologues (William Shockley), fascists like the Ku Klux Klan are armed thugs in political garb who are dedicated above all to *action*. . . ." It could appear from the above that the SYL views the racism and reaction of Wallace and the Birchites as all talk and no action. Such an illusion would constitute a serious political mistake.

If the SYL were to be logical, it would have to extend its prohibition against free speech to include not only fascists, but all capitalist officials, politicians, and parties since all are dedicated precisely to *action* (often very violent action) in defense of the racist institutions of decaying capitalism. The fascists' forthright dedication to the crushing of democratic rights, in contrast to the more cautious approach of politicians like Wallace, presents special problems to the workers' movement which are taken up in this Education for Socialists bulletin. But the SYL's argumentation hardly justifies its view that the struggle against fascism will be advanced by placing attacks on the democratic rights of fascists at the center of antifascist propaganda and action.

SYL claims to regard the San Francisco State demonstration as a "significant example" of how to fight fascism. In fact, it represents an excellent example of how *not* to fight fascist bands. Several points are worth noting in this regard.

(1) The target was not a Nazi meeting or demonstration aimed at mobilizing supporters and sympathizers, but a speech class given to inviting dissenting and "oddball" speakers. The tactics adopted should have made it clear that it was the Nazis and their racist acts, and not the rights of the assembled students to hear a particular reactionary speaker, that were the target of the protest.

(2) Instead of seeking to mobilize the kind of broad support needed for effective antifascist action, the slogans and tactics were calculated to attract a small ultraleft milieu (predominantly Maoist) which the SYL hopes to "regroup." This accounts for the contrast between the widespread

hatred for the Nazis' views and activities, and the narrowness of the so-called united front formed by the SYL. Similarly, the infantile rhetoric of these articles ("fascist feces," etc.) is aimed not at explaining the action to the many youth who have an interest in opposing fascism, but at titillating fellow ultralefts.

(3) By making "no platform for fascists" the central slogan and making opposition to free speech for fascists the primary issue, the SYL displayed the mirror image of the liberal error that was criticized in "Should Fascists Be Allowed the Right of Free Speech?" Instead of an effective countermobilization against the Nazis, the SYL indulged in an "abstract discussion over whether or not the fascist gangsters should be granted the 'democratic rights of free speech and assembly.'" Since the pivot of the action was *opposition to democratic rights for fascists* rather than *opposition to fascists because of their attacks on democratic rights*, the SYL assured that students who favored free speech for everyone and opposed Naziism would not be in the demonstration. Most of them, in fact, opposed it.

(4) By crowing about "pummeling" a few Hitlerites, the SYL helped the university administration to portray the ultraleft opponents of fascism as swaggering toughs. Physical conflicts with fascist terror gangs are inevitable in the course of the class struggle. Care should always be taken, however, that the masses understand that the issue at stake is the defense of the workers' democratic rights against fascist attacks, and not a mere "rumble" between isolated groups of "extremists." The experiences of the SWP in New York, Minneapolis, and elsewhere provide valuable examples in this regard.

(5) The description of the Nazis as "the most vicious killers of Black people" is a gross exaggeration of the present-day reality. Nazis are not the main killers of Black people today, despite their murderous actions and goals. Hundreds of Blacks are shot down each year by racist cops. Blacks in Boston face would-be lynch mobs organized by a wing of the Democratic Party. The absence of a sense of proportion in the SYL's estimate of the Nazis' role today leads to substituting small-scale fist fights with Nazis for the broader struggle against racist oppression.

(6) Having set the demonstration on an ultraleft course, the SYL was unable to control its own "well-disciplined" picket line. The SYL in this instance met a fate which has often overtaken groups that tried to recruit by outdoing "the competition" in radical posturing rather than by expressing the objective needs of the workers and their allies. They were outflanked by others who adopted a still more ultraleft stance.

(7) The outcome Marxists would have predicted for such an adventure came to pass. The ultralefts who boasted of driving the Nazis off the campus and suppressing their freedom of speech found themselves threatened with expulsion from the campus and with the suppression of their own freedom of speech. Taking advantage of the confusion produced by the ultraleft demonstration, the Nazis came back to the campus with racist leaflets slandering radicals as people who try to impose their views on the majority.

The SYL tactics gave the administration a handle for trying to suppress the left in the name of academic freedom and free speech. The *Young Spartacus* articles provide a vivid description of the SYL's isolation on the campus in the wake of its "famous victory."

The Trotskyist Young Socialist Alliance, which opposed the ultraleft action, exposed the administration's cynical effort to parade as a defender of free speech. In a leaflet distributed on campus, the San Francisco State YSA wrote:

"The Young Socialist Alliance calls for the immediate end to the victimization of student groups by the administration. The administration is using the demonstration against the Nazis on campus as a pretext to eliminate groups it wants to silence on campus.

"For the Nazis to scream that their free speech has been violated is the height of hypocrisy. The policies they advocate stand for the total elimination of free speech for Blacks, Latinos, other oppressed minorities, women, Jews and working people's organizations such as trade unions.

"For the administration to pose as defenders of free speech is hypocritical as well. It was S.I. Hayakawa (former SF State president) who tried to stop student protest by going to the lengths of disconnecting speaker wires to stop free expression. The administration consistently has denied funds for speakers they don't agree with and has attempted to restrict political literature tables on the Library plaza. The administration is more than willing to keep ROTC on campus with its recruitment and training of students for the war machine, but it is now attempting to run political organizations that oppose things like ROTC off campus.

"This victimization must be stopped. It is an attack on the democratic rights of all groups and students at S.F. State. The administration has no right to regulate student affairs.

"While the YSA did not participate in the demonstration against the Nazis and disagrees with the tactics used, we will unequivocally defend those groups involved from this administration attack. If the administration succeeds in penalizing or banning the Spartacist League, Progressive Labor Party, and the Revolutionary Student Brigade, it would be a defeat for every other student organization on campus."

Fortunately, much of the university community saw through the administration's attempt to suppress free speech in the name of free speech. The attempt to expel SYL and others was dropped. As might be expected, efforts to defend the SYL's right to free speech got far wider support than did the SYL's efforts to suppress free speech in the case of the Nazis. There is, of course, a lesson in this for those who would like to effectively mobilize mass opposition to fascism, racism, and attacks on democratic rights.

Fred Feldman
JANUARY 1976

No platform for fascist scum! SYL builds anti-Nazi demonstration

SAN FRANCISCO—On March 10 some 150 people responded to a clarion call for a mass demonstration to protest the scheduled appearance of Nazi party members on the San Francisco State University Campus. Students as well as workers from the area joined the militant picket line which was organized by the "Ad Hoc Committee to Stop the Fascists," a united front initiated and energetically built by the Spartacus Youth League. The angry demonstration not only physically confronted the Nazis but succeeded in driving the fascist vermin off campus!

The Nazis (National Socialist White People's Party) had been invited to present their "point of view" to a debate class, "Advocates and Issues," conducted by Ted Keller, a left-liberal professor. When SYL members in the class learned of the invitation, the SYL at SF State immediately launched an all-out campaign for a demonstration against the appearance of these racist killers on campus. On February 28 the SYL distributed flyers and leaflets announcing the formation of a united-front "Ad Hoc Committee to Stop the Fascists" (CSF) and calling for a meeting to plan a protest demonstration around the demand, "NO PLATFORM FOR FASCISTS!" The SYL in addition made two presentations to Keller's class strongly arguing against "free speech" for degenerate, murderous, fascist slime.

How to deal with fascists

[. . .] Unlike right-wing propaganda groups (John Birch Society), conservative bourgeois politicians (George Wallace) or reactionary academic ideologues (William Shockley), fascists like the Nazis and Ku Klux Klan are armed thugs in political garb who are dedicated above all to *action*: the genocide of racial, ethnic and religious minorities; the totalitarian suppression of bourgeois-democratic rights; and the annihilation of the organized socialist and labor movement. As long as they are still an isolated sect in this country, the Nazis sometimes pretend that they too are interested in "discussing" their "ideas." But smelling the stench of racist reaction, these scum are more brazen about raising their heads.

Excerpted from the April 1975 issue of *Young Spartacus*.

These maggots have swarmed to racially polarized Boston not to "discuss," but to foment the savage slaughter of Black schoolchildren. Nazi propaganda for frenzied white racists is a *call to action*:

"Boating, Not Busing. Or should we do some KILLING? Should we cut off, root and branch, the satanic Jews and all their lackeys who are stirring up the n_____s against us? . . . There might be school buses going up in smoke all over the country."—leaflet of National Socialist White People's Party (Bay Area). In Los Angeles recently the National Socialist Liberation Front has claimed credit for attacking leftist bookstores. Their "argument": dynamite.

Fascist movements grow not through political campaigning but through terror, murder, and eventually concentration camps and gas chambers. The Nazis win their arguments with blood and prove their points with genocide. They yearn for the day when they can exterminate their opponents and victims. We recognize no democratic rights for Nazis. There is nothing to debate with these racist monsters! Action must be met with action! The Nazis must be stopped!

As the Trotskyist *Transitional Program* spells out so forcefully, only a united, militant labor-led mobilization can deal decisively with the racist swine:

"The struggle against fascism does not start in the liberal editorial office but in the factory—and ends in the street. . . . In connection with every strike and street demonstration, it is imperative to propagate the necessity of creating *workers' groups for self-defense*. It is necessary to write this slogan into the program of the revolutionary wing of the trade unions. . . . It is necessary to advance the slogan of a workers *militia* as the one serious guarantee for the inviolability of workers' organizations, meetings, and press." It is necessary, again in the words of the *Transitional Program*, "to inflict a series of tactical defeats upon the armed thugs of counterrevolution." Depending upon the relationship of forces, left organizations or groups of militants in certain situations may correctly decide to take upon themselves the suppression of fascist meetings and demonstrations. But Communists must dissuade anti-fascist militants from adventurist confrontationism which substitutes for the necessary perspective of struggling to mobilize the masses against the fascists.

We warn that no confidence should be placed in the bosses' cops to restrain or stop the fascist bands. [. . .] Reliance upon the cops to restrain or stop the fascist bands is an invitation to murder. These racist killers must be made to fear the consequences of creeping forth and spewing their poison!

United front gathers support

[. . .] In addition to the Spartacist League/SYL, endorsements were obtained from the Committee for Working Class Studies, Socialist League (Democratic Centralist), Laney College Black Student Union [Oakland], Center for Peace and Social Justice, Service Employees Union Local 411 (the SF State campus workers union), Committee for a Militant UAW/Local 1364, Militant Action Caucus of the CWA, the Militant Caucus/Local 6 and *Longshore Militant*/Local 10 of the ILWU, as well as individual, recognized labor militants.

The other self-proclaimed "socialist" organizations on campus responded to the principled united-front call of the growing CSF with either sectarian adventurism or cowardly abstentionism. The muddled Stalinites of the Progressive Labor Party (PL) did vigorously campaign in their own name to prevent the fascists from speaking on campus. Opposed to joining in united-front actions with Trotskyists, PL attempted to outmaneuver the CSF with hyper-militant rhetorical oneupmanship. [. . .]

Although the hardened reformists of the Socialist Workers Party/Young Socialist Alliance (SWP/YSA) crow about opposing racism and fighting for civil rights, these cynical ex-Trotskyists are presently interested only in organizing respectable, pacifist conventions and desultory rallies for liberal politicians and bourgeois-legalistic organizations such as the NAACP. In the past the SWP/YSA liquidated into the various petty-bourgeois radical protest movements, declaring that "consistent" studentism, feminism and nationalism equal socialism. Lately, however, the line of the SWP/YSA appears to be that "consistent" Uncle Tom liberalism equals socialism!

Thus, it should come as no surprise that these "socialists" simply ignored the campaign against the Nazis, the most vicious killers of Black people. The problem with the "ostrich position," comrades of the SWP/YSA, is that when you stick your head in the sand, another part of your anatomy is quite prominent.

The feminists of the Women's center at SF State refused to endorse the CSF, because a demonstration against the Nazis, whose slogan for women is *Kinder, Kuche, Kirche* (children, the kitchen, the church), is supposedly a "male" tactic! The Pan Africanists, according to one of their members on campus, said they would let the whites fight it out. Their nationalism prevents the Pan Africanists from following the example of their black brothers at the University of North Carolina in Chapel Hill who mobilized and prevented KKK leader David Duke from performing there in January.

CSF leads militant demonstration
The anti-Nazi demonstration called by the CSF drew some 150 students and workers into a well-disciplined picket line in front of the building where the Nazis were scheduled to appear. To their credit, supporters of PL joined the picket line, but the Revolutionary Student Brigade held its "own" tiny rally about 200 yards away. In order to protect its sub-reformist politics from any criticism or competing program, the RSB resorts to such theatrical self-exclusionism.

After the demonstration had been in progress for about 45 minutes and the Nazis still were nowhere in sight, some elements, who had refused to join the united-front steering committee, suddenly announced over a bullhorn that the demonstration should enter the building. This splitting tactic was irresponsible in the extreme, since a large number of people packed into the narrow corridors and small classroom would virtually be unable to physically defend themselves should there be an attack by the Nazis and cops.

The steering committee advised these demonstrators against such an ill-considered tactic, but nonetheless many students entered the building. They crowded into the corridor and packed Keller's classroom, beginning what was to be a several-hours long debate with Keller and the students in the class awaiting the Nazis. Keller announced that the Nazis would not appear and the class was canceled.

When it was announced sometime later that the Nazis still had not arrived, the large SYL contingent left the area to go directly to the Berkeley campus for an anti-ROTC demonstration scheduled for 2 p.m.

Racist filth found
The dwindling crowd inside the building continued the antifascist chanting and arguments with the students who recognized the Nazis' "right" of free speech. The comings and goings of the press soon attracted their attention, and a rumor that the Nazis were somewhere in the building began to circulate.

Investigation soon revealed that in fact the fascists were in the building, hiding in a nearby office! [. . .]

The remaining group of demonstrators rushed to the room and began to pound on the barricaded door. A squad of campus and local cops were protecting the seven fascists inside. After some time, the door suddenly opened and the Nazis, surrounded by a beefy cordon of pushing cops, made a bee line for their getaway van, waiting nearby with the motor running.

Fortunately, several students were able to land a few blows to the scurrying rodents, and one was even flattened out on the pavement. In the melee one of these thugs clubbed a student with a portable fire extinguisher and then sprayed its chemical contents into his face. Only with the eager aid of a rearguard of club swinging cops were the fascists able to pile into their van and execute their escape.

Administration prepares for repression
For the next several days the campus and local press were filled with coverage, photographs and editorials on the demonstration. The SF State administration as well as some faculty and students have raised a hue and cry over the denial of "free speech" to the Nazis by the CSF and others. SF President Romberg has already begun an "investigation" into the demonstration, and the Faculty Academic Senate and Associated Students Judicial Committee have announced that they may hold hearings. Even Professor Keller has issued a 12(!)-page polemical attack on the SYL and PL which is strongly tinged with anticommunism.

The Dean of Student Affairs on March 17 sent

letters to every student registered in the "Issues and Advocacy" class, soliciting "a statement which you feel may be helpful to us in our endeavor to prevent the interference of academic freedom." A formal complaint has already been filed against the SYL and PL with the Judicial Committee. Anti-left petitions are circulating and the Academic Freedom Committee has released a formal statement condemning the action. The administration is clearly preparing to attempt to prosecute and ban the SYL and PL.

The SYL issued a leaflet the day following the demonstration which strongly solidarized with the effort to pummel the fascists: "The entire Bay Area workers' movement should applaud the efforts of the students here at State for teaching the Nazis this well deserved lesson." We declared that: "The Spartacus Youth League is glad to accept responsibility as the initiators of the Ad Hoc Committee to Stop the Fascists which set up the picket line demonstration". [. . .]

No reprisals!

The SYL has stood firm in the face of threatened repression and has initiated the "March 10 Defense Committee" to fight any reprisals taken against anyone—excluding the Nazis—charged in connection with the antifascist demonstration. Two administrators from the student affairs department attended the first defense meeting and indicated they would not provide the SF State administration with any information that could potentially implicate any student in the demonstration. The SYL has held a forum on campus, has begun circulating a petition demanding no reprisals and has sent letters to scores of Bay Area trade unions appealing for support in the defense campaign. Professor Keller signed the defense petition and told SYL members that he plans to write a statement opposing reprisals. In the coming weeks the SYL will show the anti-fascist film about gruesome Nazi atrocities, "Night and Fog," as one means to build for a demonstration on campus. NO REPRISALS!

Defense of anti-Nazi demonstrators scores victory!

"If the enemy had known how weak we were, it would probably have reduced us to jelly. . . . It would have crushed in blood the very beginning of our work."
                    Goebbels

San Francisco—A concerted attempt by the administration of San Francisco State University (SFS) to purge organizations charged with "disruption" in connection with the militant demonstration that drove the Nazis off campus on March 10 has been thwarted. The successful anti-Nazi demonstration and the aggressive, resourceful defense campaign, for both of which the Spartacus Youth League was centrally responsible, stand as significant examples for left-wing activists, who increasingly will come face-to-face with the fascists and other right-wing goons.

On May 6 Associate Dean of Students Sandra Duffield ruled that "no action should be taken regarding the groups allegedly or admittedly involved" in the antifascist demonstration, namely the SYL, Progressive Labor Party and the Revolutionary Student Brigade. The ruling was made on the basis of the recommendation by the Organizational Review Committee that "no action be taken against any group named."

Both the ORC recommendation and the Duffield decision, however, maintain that a "disruption" occurred and reaffirm the "right" of the fascist scum to "free speech" on campus in the future. Both assert that such "disruptions" should be prevented by ensuring that cops are mobilized on campus for any future demonstrations. With this warning, the administration has backed off from pursuing the witchhunt. However, one of the students who originally filed charges against the SYL, PL and the RSB has now stated his intention to appeal the Duf-

Excerpted from the June 1975 issue of *Young Spartacus*.

field decision. Whether or not the administration will choose to renew its campaign against the left through this appeal is not at this time clear. While Duffield has spoken unsympathetically of the appeal, the Dean of Student Affairs, responsible for making a ruling in the case of such an appeal, has not yet released a statement. This Dean was one of the first to denounce the March 10 demonstration as a "disruption" and was responsible for initiating the "investigation" into the action.

Militants demonstrate, fascists cower

The so-called "disruption" on March 10 was the outcome of a militant demonstration by 100–150 students, faculty and trade unionists which had been called by the Ad Hoc Committee to Stop the Fascists, a united front initiated by the SYL around the demand, "No Platform for Fascists!" [. . .] Unfortunately having been invited to make a "presentation" to a speech class, "Advocacy and Issues," the fascist feces dared not to appear before the class and instead cowered in a nearby office, spewing their filth to reporters seeking a sensationalist story.

When the demonstrators discovered their lair, the cops arrived and tried to escort these aspiring SS men to their waiting army surplus truck. Several of the fleeing rodents were pummeled by angry demonstrators before they were able to make their getaway under cop protection.

In a statement distributed at SF State the following day the SYL solidarized with the "education" given the Nazis, declaring: "This is just as it should be. There is no legitimate platform for would-be Hitlers. The abstract question of 'free speech' to such small-time petty thugs is clearly subordinate to the class question of defense of minorities and the labor movement as a whole." Communists and labor militants recognize no democratic rights for fascists, who terrorize and murder black people today and who would stoke ovens with mountains of corpses should they rise to power. The leaflet went on to caution that the administration might well seize upon the "disruption" to attempt reprisals against the campus left involved in the action.

Witchhunt

The administration began quickly to begin whipping up an atmosphere for a witch hunt of student radicals. Within hours of the demonstration, SFS President Romberg issued a public statement which thundered, "We will not tolerate the destruction of academic freedom at San Francisco State University by an organization which denies the reasonable exercise of free speech by others." Two days later, Romberg's lackey, Dean of Humanities Leo Young, brought formal charges against the Spartacus Youth League, PL, RSB and the Jewish Lesbian Gang, demanding that they be barred from campus, quite a denial of "free speech"! The Dean of Student Affairs then rushed out letters to all students registered in the class requesting them to fink on the demonstrators.

The bourgeois media likewise fully backed up the witchhunting administration. The *San Francisco Chronicle* (March 12) vented its spleen on the demonstrators in an editorial that equated the protestors with the fascists. Other papers and radio stations blared shrill editorials hypocritically ranting about "free speech" and the U.S. Constitution.

On campus, hostility to the demonstration was also widespread, even affecting many students who considered themselves to be left-wing radicals. For several weeks the campus newspaper was deluged with letters denouncing the denial of "free speech" to the Nazis—more accurately, to anyone, including the Nazis. The letters particularly criticized the SYL, the recognized leader of the united-front demonstration.

SYL initiates defense campaign

As soon as the charges became public, the SYL began to organize the March 10 Defense Committee (M10) as a united front based on the slogans, "Stop the Witchhunt!, Drop the Charges!, No Reprisals!" The M10 Committee held a press conference, at which attorney Charles Garry, Charles Jackson (former activist in the SFS Black Student Union), several trade-union militants, and a representative of the SYL spoke.

The M10 Committee held fund-raising events, notably the showing of the film "Night and Fog," which depicts the sickening horrors of Nazi barbarism in searing images that shatter pedantic, academic disputations on the "moral right" of the fascists to "free speech." The SYL also held forums on campus pedagogically explaining the nature of fascist movements and the working-class strategy to defeat fascism.

Before an audience of over 150 students and faculty the SYL debated the proposition "No Platform for Fascists" with the liberal professors Keller and McGuckin who were responsible for inviting the Nazi swine on campus. Against the pervasive liberal attitude on campus, most articulately voiced by Keller and McGuckin, that fascism can be defeated in the "free marketplace of ideas," the SYL in one of its several special *Young Spartacus* supplements argued:

"Fascism is a military phenomenon. It cannot be defeated through polemical struggle. We didn't organize on March 10 around 'No Platform for Fascists' because we stand in fear of fascist 'ideas'. [. . .] Rather, we refuse to wait until the fascists get strong enough to carry out their terrorist program, possibly taking the precious lives of some workers and leftists, before we act against it." [. . .]

The "respectable" YSA, which had done absolutely nothing to protest the appearance of the Nazis on campus, echoed the wail of the liberals and smeared the militant demonstration as "unfortunate," "counterproductive," and even a "disruption." These tongue-clicking "Trotskyists" lecture that fascism should be discouraged through "an educational campaign" (*Zengers*, March 10, 1975)! But when it came to defending the left under administration attack, the YSA flounced out of the M10 Committee and did absolutely nothing, not even an "educational campaign," to beat back the witch-hunt. [. . .]

DEFENDING WORKERS' RIGHTS

Socialism on Trial
TESTIMONY AT MINNEAPOLIS SEDITION TRIAL
James P. Cannon

The revolutionary program of the working class, presented in response to frame-up charges of "seditious conspiracy" in 1941, on the eve of US entry into World War II. The defendants were leaders of the Minneapolis labor movement and the Socialist Workers Party. $15. Also in Spanish, French, Farsi.

Cointelpro
THE FBI'S SECRET WAR ON POLITICAL FREEDOM
Nelson Blackstock

An in-depth look at the 1960s and '70s covert FBI disruption and counterintelligence program—code-named COINTELPRO. Contains reproductions of FBI documents released through the Socialist Workers Party suit against government spying. $15

50 Years of Covert Operations in the US
WASHINGTON'S POLITICAL POLICE AND THE AMERICAN WORKING CLASS
Larry Seigle, Farrell Dobbs, Steve Clark

How class-conscious workers have defended constitutional freedoms and fought the capitalists' drive to build the "national security" state essential to maintaining their rule. $10. Also in Spanish and Farsi.

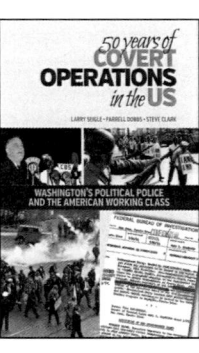

FBI on Trial
THE VICTORY IN THE SOCIALIST WORKERS PARTY SUIT AGAINST GOVERNMENT SPYING
Margaret Jayko

The record of a historic victory in the fight for political rights, including the 1986 federal court ruling against government spying and excerpts from trial testimony by SWP leaders Farrell Dobbs and Jack Barnes. $17

PATHFINDERPRESS.COM

WORKING-CLASS LEADERSHIP AND THE SOCIALIST REVOLUTION

New Edition!
Che Guevara on Economics and Politics in the Transition to Socialism
CARLOS TABLADA

It's essential for working people to win state power, said Ernesto Che Guevara. "Then there's the second stage, maybe more difficult than the first"—the transition from dog-eat-dog capitalism to socialism. That includes moving from work as a condition for survival, to voluntary social labor through which we express our common humanity. Includes Fidel Castro's 1987 speech "Che's Ideas are Absolutely Relevant Today." New edition with substantially expanded selections from Guevara's writings. $17. Also in Spanish, coming in French.

Lenin's Final Fight
Speeches and Writings, 1922–23
V.I. LENIN

In 1922 and 1923, V.I. Lenin, central leader of the world's first socialist revolution, waged what was to be his last political battle—one that was lost after his death. At stake was whether that revolution, and the international communist movement it led, would remain on the revolutionary proletarian course that brought workers and peasants to power in October 1917. $17. Also in Spanish, Farsi, Greek.

The Challenge of the Left Opposition
LEON TROTSKY

Continuing the political fight V.I. Lenin began at the end of his life, Leon Trotsky explains that "our task is the rebirth of Bolshevik politics within the parties of the Communist International." Three volumes record the struggle Trotsky led in the 1920s to defend Lenin's proletarian internationalist course. $25 each

In Defense of Socialism
Four Speeches on the 30th Anniversary of the Cuban Revolution, 1988–89
FIDEL CASTRO

Castro describes the decisive place of volunteer Cuban fighters in the war in Angola against invading forces of South Africa's apartheid regime. Not only is economic and social progress possible without capitalism's dog-eat-dog relations, the Cuban leader says, but socialism is humanity's only way forward. $12. Also in Greek.

The Revolution Betrayed
What Is the Soviet Union and Where Is It Going?
LEON TROTSKY

In 1917 workers and peasants of Russia were the motor force of one of the deepest revolutions in history. Yet within ten years a political counterrevolution by a privileged social layer, whose chief spokesperson was Joseph Stalin, was being consolidated. The classic study of the Soviet workers state and its degeneration. $17. Also in Spanish, Farsi, Greek.

Colombia: Fidel Castro on the Debate around Revolutionary Strategy and Lessons of the Cuban Revolution
FROM THE PAGES OF THE *MILITANT*

Fidel Castro describes the Cuban leadership's efforts to end decades of war between the FARC guerrilla movement and Colombia's brutal regime. He explains why Cuban revolutionaries, unlike FARC leaders, rejected taking hostages and organized Cuba's working people to win state power, not pursue a "prolonged people's war." $5. Also in Spanish.

Essential Works of Lenin

Contains *What Is to Be Done?* as well as *State and Revolution* and *Imperialism: The Highest Stage of Capitalism*. $17

CAPITALIST CRISIS AND THE FIGHT FOR WORKERS POWER

The Transitional Program for Socialist Revolution
LEON TROTSKY

The Socialist Workers Party program, drafted by Trotsky in 1938, still guides the SWP and communists the world over. The party "uncompromisingly gives battle to all political groupings tied to the apron strings of the bourgeoisie. Its task—the abolition of capitalism's domination. Its aim—socialism. Its method—the proletarian revolution." $17. Also in Farsi.

Is Socialist Revolution in the US Possible?
A Necessary Debate among Working People
MARY-ALICE WATERS

Fighting for a society only working people can create, it is our own capacities we will discover. And we will answer the question posed here with a resounding "Yes." Revolution is possible but not inevitable. That depends on us. $7. Also in Spanish, French, Farsi.

Labor, Nature, and the Evolution of Humanity
The Long View of History
FREDERICK ENGELS, KARL MARX, GEORGE NOVACK, MARY-ALICE WATERS

Without understanding that social labor, transforming nature, has driven humanity's evolution for millions of years, working people are unable to see beyond the capitalist epoch of class exploitation that warps all human relations, ideas, and values. Only the revolutionary conquest of state power by the working class can open the door to a world free of capitalist exploitation, degradation of nature, subjugation of women, racism, and war. A world built on human solidarity. A socialist world. $12. Also in Spanish and French.

Imperialism's March toward Fascism and War
JACK BARNES

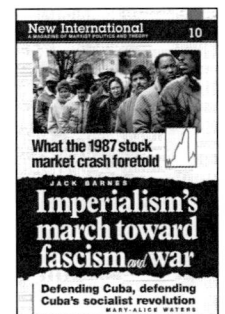

"There will be new Hitlers, new Mussolinis. That is inevitable. What is not inevitable is that they will triumph. The working-class vanguard will organize our class to fight back against the devastating toll we are made to pay for the capitalist crisis. The future of humanity will be decided in the contest between these contending class forces." In *New International* no. 10. $14. Also in Spanish, French, Farsi, Greek.

Cuba and the Coming American Revolution
JACK BARNES

This is a book about the example set by the Cuban people that revolution is not only necessary—it can be made. A book about the struggles of workers and other exploited producers in the imperialist heartland, and the youth attracted to them. About the class struggle in the US, where the revolutionary capacities of working people are as utterly discounted by the ruling powers as were those of the Cuban toilers. And just as wrongly. $10. Also in Spanish, French, Farsi.

Teamster Rebellion
FARRELL DOBBS

The 1934 strikes that won union recognition for truckers and warehouse workers in Minneapolis and helped pave the way for the working-class social movement that built the industrial unions. The first of four volumes by a central leader of these battles. $16. Also in Spanish, French, Farsi, Greek.

The Communist Manifesto
KARL MARX AND FREDERICK ENGELS

Communism, say the founding leaders of the revolutionary workers movement, is not a set of ideas or preconceived "principles" but workers' line of march to power, springing from a "movement going on under our very eyes." $5. Also in Spanish, French, Farsi, Arabic.

PATHFINDERPRESS.COM

EXPAND YOUR REVOLUTIONARY LIBRARY

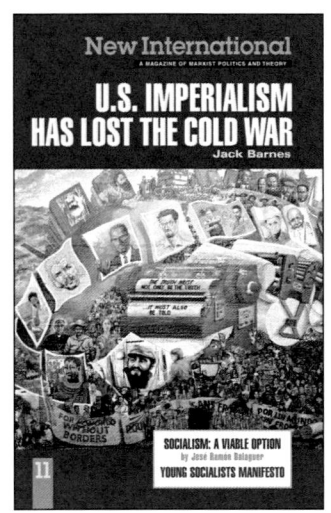

U.S. Imperialism Has Lost the Cold War
JACK BARNES

The collapse of regimes across Eastern Europe and the USSR claiming to be communist did not mean workers and farmers there had been crushed. In today's sharpening class conflicts and wars, these toilers are joining working people the world over in the class struggle against capitalist exploitation. In *New International* no. 11. $14. Also in Spanish, French, Farsi, Greek.

The Struggle against Fascism in Germany
LEON TROTSKY

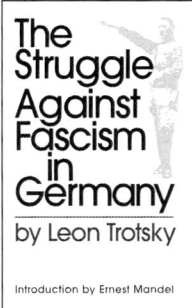

Writing in the heat of struggle against the rising Nazi movement, a central leader of the Bolshevik Revolution in Russia draws lessons from that first victorious proletarian revolution, examines the petty bourgeois class roots of fascism, and presents a revolutionary political course to defeat it. $25

Fascism and Big Business
DANIEL GUERIN

Examines the development of fascism in Germany and Italy and its relationship with the ruling capitalist families there. $20

Women in Cuba: The Making of a Revolution within the Revolution
VILMA ESPÍN, ASELA DE LOS SANTOS YOLANDA FERRER

The integration of women in the ranks and leadership of the Cuban Revolution was intertwined with the proletarian course of the leadership of the revolution from the start. This is the story of that revolution and how it transformed the women and men who made it. $17. Also in Spanish, Farsi, Greek.

The First and Second Declarations of Havana

Nowhere are the questions of revolutionary strategy that today confront men and women on the front lines of struggles in the Americas addressed with greater truthfulness and clarity than in these uncompromising indictments of imperialist plunder and "the exploitation of man by man." Adopted by million-strong assemblies of the Cuban people in 1960 and 1962. $10. Also in Spanish, French, Farsi, Arabic, Greek.

Thomas Sankara Speaks
The Burkina Faso Revolution, 1983–87

Under Sankara's guidance, Burkina Faso's revolutionary government led peasants, workers, women, and youth to expand literacy; to sink wells, plant trees, erect housing; to combat women's oppression; to carry out land reform; to join others worldwide to free themselves from the imperialist yoke. $20. Also in French.

Pathfinder Press accessible ebooks for the blind, those with low vision, or other challenges reading print books

For a list of current accessible titles, go to: pathfinderpress.com/collections/books-for-the-blind.

Visit Bookshare.org for information on how to sign up.

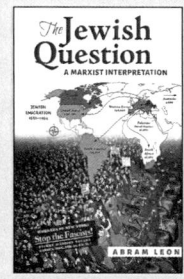